167 EPIC WORLD WAR 1 FACTS

The Ultimate Collection of Shocking WWI Stories and Little-Known History to Test Your Knowledge and Win Trivia Night

SCOTT MATTHEWS

The more that you read, the more things you will know. The more you learn, the more places you'll go.

- Dr. Seuss

Contents

Introduction

In the early years of the twentieth century, much of the world believed it was entering a new age of progress.

Cities were growing fast. Trains crossed continents. Telegraph wires carried messages in minutes instead of weeks. Electricity lit streets that had once gone dark at sunset. Medicine was improving. Industry was booming. Empires felt confident, modern, and powerful.

To many people living in Europe in 1914, war felt like an outdated idea. Something from the past. Nations had fought before, of course, but the belief was that modern diplomacy, technology, and shared culture would prevent anything truly catastrophic.

They were wrong.

Beneath the surface, the world was tightly wound.

Countries had spent decades building massive armies and navies, convinced that strength alone would guarantee safety. Military plans were drawn up years in advance, timed to railway schedules and mobilization orders that could not easily be slowed or stopped. Alliances bound nations together so rigidly that a conflict between two countries could pull in half the world within days.

National pride ran hot. Old rivalries simmered. Borders were disputed.

Empires feared decline. Politicians made promises they could not easily back away from.

The system looked stable, but it was brittle.

All it needed was a spark.

In June of 1914, that spark appeared in the city of Sarajevo. A single assassination, carried out in a crowded street, set off a chain reaction no one could fully control. Within weeks, Europe's great powers were issuing ultimatums, mobilizing armies, and declaring war.

Many believed it would be over quickly.

Young men rushed to enlist. Some smiled for photographs. Some treated it like an adventure. Newspapers spoke of glory, honor, and decisive victories. Soldiers packed light, expecting to return home within months.

Instead, the world fell into a war unlike anything it had ever seen.

World War I was not a war of sweeping cavalry charges and heroic duels. It became a war of trenches carved into mud, stretching for hundreds of miles. A war where machine guns could cut down entire units in seconds. Where artillery shells fell day and night, sometimes for weeks without pause.

It was the first truly industrial war.

New technologies appeared almost as quickly as soldiers could adapt to them. Poison gas drifted across battlefields. Submarines hunted unseen beneath the sea. Airplanes, once a novelty, became weapons of war.

Millions of soldiers lived underground like animals, surrounded by rats, lice, and constant fear. Civilians far from the front lines were pulled into the conflict through rationing, propaganda, forced labor, and bombing raids. Entire societies were reshaped by the demands of total war.

And when it finally ended, the cost was staggering.

More than sixteen million people were dead. Entire empires had collapsed. Borders were redrawn. Families were shattered. The psychological wounds would last for generations. The world that emerged afterward was not safer or more stable, but fragile, angry, and unsettled.

In many ways, the modern world was born in the trenches of World War I.

This book is not a traditional history lesson.

It does not move carefully year by year or battle by battle. It does not ask you to memorize dates, maps, or lists of generals. Instead, it focuses on the moments that reveal what this war truly was.

The strange facts.

The brutal realities.

The human stories.

The overlooked details that textbooks often skip.

You'll hear about soldiers, spies, nurses, and civilians. About inventions created out of desperation. About decisions that changed history in ways no one intended. About courage, fear, ingenuity, and unimaginable loss.

Some facts will surprise you.

Some will disturb you.

Some will change how you think about war entirely.

Each stands on its own, but together they paint a picture of a conflict that reshaped the world in ways we are still living with today.

This is not just a story about how World War I began.

It is a collection of moments that show what happened when a modern world collided with industrialized violence for the first time.

This is *Epic World War I Facts*.

ONE

World War One

1. The Assassination That Sparked World War I

On a bright, hot Sunday in June 1914, a man named Archduke Franz Ferdinand was riding through the streets of Sarajevo in an open-top car. He was a powerful man, the heir to a massive empire, and he was dressed in his finest military uniform, complete with a hat decorated with green feathers. Beside him sat his wife, Sophie. It was their wedding anniversary, and despite the political tension in the air, they wanted to show the people they were friendly and unafraid.

But hiding in the crowds were six young men with a dark plan. They were nationalists who wanted their people to be free from the Archduke's empire, and they had come armed with bombs and pistols. Earlier that morning, one of them had already thrown a bomb at the car. It missed, bouncing off the folded-back roof and exploding under the car behind them, injuring several people. Most people would have fled the city right then, but the Archduke was stubborn. He insisted on going to the hospital to visit the people who had been hurt.

This is where history took a strange and deadly turn. The Archduke's drivers weren't told about the change in plans. As the motorcade sped through the city, the lead driver took a wrong turn onto a narrow side street. When the Archduke's driver realized the mistake, he slammed on the brakes to try and reverse. The engine stalled, and the heavy car came to a jerky stop right in front of a deli.

Standing outside that deli was nineteen-year-old Gavrilo Princip. He had been part of the assassination plot earlier that morning and thought he had failed. He was likely standing there wondering what to do next when, suddenly, his target literally stopped right in front of him. Princip didn't hesitate. He stepped toward the car and fired two shots from just a few feet away. One bullet hit the Archduke in the neck, and the other hit Sophie.

In the chaos that followed, the Archduke's last words were a plea to his wife: *"Sophie, Sophie! Don't die! Live for our children!"* But it was too late. By the time the car reached help, both were dead. Those two small pieces of lead didn't just kill a couple on their anniversary; they acted like a spark in a room full of gunpowder. Because of the complicated promises different countries had made to protect one another, this one local tragedy began to pull the entire world into a war that no one truly knew how to stop.

2. The Rivalries and Alliances Behind World War I

To understand why a single shooting in a far-off city could set the whole world on fire, you have to look at Europe like a giant playground full of bullies and nervous friends who had all made secret pacts with one another. By 1914, the continent was split into two main "teams." On one side was the Triple Entente, made up of Britain, France, and Russia. On the other side was the Triple Alliance, which included Germany, Austria-Hungary, and Italy. These weren't just friendly handshakes; they were "all-or-nothing" promises. If one country got into a fight, their partners were forced to jump in and help, whether they wanted to or not.

The biggest "bully" on the block was Germany. It was a relatively new country, but it was growing incredibly fast. They had the best factories, a massive army, and they were starting to build a navy that made Britain, the king of the seas, very worried. Germany felt surrounded by enemies and believed that the only way to be safe was to be the strongest. Meanwhile, France was still bitter and angry over a war they had lost to Germany forty years earlier. They wanted their land back and were looking for any excuse to take it. Then there was Russia, a massive but struggling empire that saw itself as the "big brother" to smaller Slavic nations like Serbia.

Adding to the tension was the race for "Empires." The powerful countries of Europe were like collectors, trying to grab as much land as possible in Africa and Asia. They wanted the gold, the rubber, and the glory that came with owning colonies. This made everyone suspicious of everyone else. If France took a piece of land in Africa, Germany felt they had to take two pieces just to keep up. It was a never-ending competition that made every border in Europe feel like a tripwire.

By the time 1914 rolled around, these countries weren't just talking about war; they were preparing for it with industrial precision. They had built thousands of miles of special railways just to move soldiers to the front lines. They had filled warehouses with millions of uniforms and rifles. Every general had a "plan" tucked away in a desk drawer, a step-by-step guide on how to invade their neighbors. The atmosphere was so thick with distrust that people started calling Europe a "powder keg." It was a room filled with gunpowder, and all the leaders were walking around holding lit matches, hoping they wouldn't be the one to drop theirs first.

3. Germany's Plan for a Two-Front War

Once the alliances were triggered and the "Great Rush" of soldiers began, the generals finally got to use the secret plans they had been perfecting for decades. The most famous and dangerous of these was Germany's Schlieffen Plan. The German leaders were terrified of a "two-front war," the idea of having to fight the massive Russian army in the East and the powerful French army in the West at the exact same time. It would be like a person trying to fight off two different attackers from opposite sides. To avoid this, they decided they had to knock France out of the war in just six weeks, before the slow-moving Russian "steamroller" could even get its boots on.

To make this work, the German army didn't march straight toward the heavily defended French border. Instead, they swung like a giant hammer through the neutral, peaceful country of Belgium. This move shocked the world. Belgium was a small nation that just wanted to be left alone, but the German plan required their flat roads and railways to get to Paris quickly. This "rape of Belgium," as the newspapers called it, changed the politics of the war instantly. It turned the conflict from a local dispute into a moral crusade. In London, the British government, which had been hesitating, now felt it had no choice but to enter the war to protect the "sanctity of small nations."

As the German "hammer" swung through Belgium and into Northern France, the maps in the war rooms of Paris and London were covered in red ink. The French army, dressed in outdated bright blue coats and red trousers, suffered staggering losses as they tried to stop the grey-clad German tide. By September 1914, the Germans were so close to Paris that the French government fled the city, and the sound of German heavy guns could be heard by civilians in the streets. It looked like the war might actually be over by Christmas, just as everyone had predicted, but with a German victory.

Then came the Battle of the Marne, a moment that changed everything. In a desperate, last-ditch effort, the French and British managed to find a gap in the German lines. They threw everything they had into the fight. The German advance was finally halted. Exhausted and running out of supplies, the German army retreated a few miles and did something no one expected: they dug in. They shoveled out long, shallow ditches to protect themselves from the deadly machine-gun fire. The Allies did the same. Within weeks, these simple ditches began to stretch and grow, forming a solid line of earthworks that would eventually run from the sea all the way to the mountains. The "War of Movement" was over, and the era of the trench had begun.

4. The Race to the Sea and the Birth of Trench Warfare

By the late autumn of 1914, the grand plans for a quick victory had vanished into the damp earth of Northern France. After the massive movements of the summer, both the Allied and German armies found themselves in a desperate situation. Neither side could move forward against the power of modern rifles and heavy guns, so they began a frantic series of maneuvers that historians call the "Race to the Sea." This was a high-stakes game of leapfrog on a continental scale. Each army tried to outflank the other, moving further and further north toward the coast of Belgium, hoping to find an open path to get behind the enemy lines. But at every turn, they found their path blocked by fresh troops and ready defenses.

When they finally reached the cold waters of the North Sea, there was nowhere left to run. The two massive forces were now locked in a line that stretched for hundreds of miles, from the sandy beaches of the coast all the way to the rugged mountains of the Swiss border. To stay alive in this open landscape, the soldiers did the only thing they could. They used their small shovels to dig shallow holes in the dirt. Over the following weeks, these holes were connected and deepened, turning into a permanent system of earthworks that would not move significantly for the next four years. This was the moment the world realized that the war had changed from a contest of speed and skill into a static, industrial struggle.

In the grand palaces and government buildings of London, Paris, and Berlin, the mood shifted from excitement to a heavy, calculated determination. The leaders had to accept that the "short war" they had promised was an illusion. This political realization led to a massive change in how nations were run. They began to look at the map not as a series of battlefields, but as a giant balance sheet of resources. They needed more coal, more steel, and more men than anyone had ever imagined. The home fronts were now just as important as the front lines, and the governments began to take total control over every aspect of civilian life to keep the war machine running.

The birth of this continuous line of defenses created a new and strange reality for the world. For the first time in history, two of the most powerful military forces ever assembled were staring at each other across a narrow strip of wasted land, unable to move. This stalemate forced the scientists and the generals to start looking for new, more terrifying ways to break the deadlock. The war was no longer about who had the best cavalry or the bravest chargers. It was now a cold, political battle of endurance. As the first winter of the war approached, the world was settling into a long, dark period of waiting, and the hope of a quick resolution was replaced by the grim reality of a struggle that would consume an entire generation.

5. The War Expands Beyond Europe

As the year 1915 opened, the war underwent a massive transformation that pulled the map of the conflict far beyond the borders of Europe. The most significant political shift occurred when the Ottoman Empire decided to join the side of Germany and Austria-Hungary. This decision was a strategic earthquake for the Allied powers. Suddenly, the British and French had to worry about their vast interests in the Middle East and the safety of the Suez Canal, which was the vital artery connecting Britain to its colonies in India and Australia. The war was no longer just a struggle over the fields of France; it had become a contest for the control of the ancient world and the vast oil resources that were beginning to drive modern industry.

The entry of the Ottoman Empire opened up several new and difficult fronts that required the Allies to divert hundreds of thousands of soldiers away from the Western Front. In the rugged, freezing mountains of the Caucasus, the Russians found themselves locked in a brutal struggle against the Ottoman forces. Meanwhile, in the hot, dusty plains of Mesopotamia and the deserts of the Sinai, British and colonial troops began a long campaign to protect the edges of their empire. These new theaters of war were incredibly challenging because they required different types of supplies, different clothing, and a different kind of endurance. The high-level planners in London and Paris were forced to juggle multiple crises at once, stretching their navies and their logistics to the breaking point.

This expansion of the war also had a profound effect on the global political atmosphere. It turned the conflict into a truly world-wide struggle between different types of empires. In the big cities of the Middle East, such as Cairo and Baghdad, the arrival of modern war brought a sense of upheaval and change that would eventually redraw the borders of the entire region. The British and French began to make secret promises to various local groups, hoping to stir up internal rebellions against the Ottomans. These political maneuvers were designed to win the war, but they were also planting the seeds for future conflicts that would last for a century.

By the middle of 1915, the "Bird's Eye View" of the war showed a world that was becoming increasingly entangled. The oceans were now just as dangerous as the land, as the German U-boats began to target merchant ships in an attempt to cut off the flow of supplies to the Allies. The conflict had become a giant, interconnected system where a battle in a desert could affect the food prices in a European city. The leaders of the major powers realized that they were no longer just fighting a war of armies, but a war of entire systems. Every corner of the globe was being pulled into the gravity of the conflict, and the hope of a local, contained resolution had completely vanished.

6. The Dominions and the Rise of the ANZAC Spirit

To understand the global scale of the war in 1915, you have to look at the unique and powerful bond that tied the people of Australia, New Zealand, and Canada to the British Isles. At the time, these countries were not just allies; they were Dominions of the British Empire, and most of their citizens still viewed Britain as the "mother country." Many families had only emigrated a generation or two earlier, and their sense of identity was deeply rooted in British culture, law, and history. When the King declared war in London, the people in Melbourne and Toronto felt as though their own homes were under threat. There was a widespread belief that if the heart of the empire fell, their own young nations would be left defenseless in a dangerous world.

The motivations for these young men to join the "Great Rush" were a complex mix of duty, adventure, and a desire to prove themselves on the world stage. In Australia and New Zealand, there was a feeling that their countries were still "children" in the eyes of the world, and that by fighting alongside the great powers, they would finally earn their place as mature, independent nations. For a young man in the Australian outback or the Canadian wilderness, the war was a chance to escape a quiet life of hard labor and see the legendary cities of the old world. They joined because they were told the empire was in danger, but they also joined because they wanted to be part of the greatest event in human history. They were often the tallest, healthiest, and most enthusiastic soldiers on the battlefield, and they brought a sense of rugged confidence that stood in stark contrast to the exhausted armies of Europe.

This loyalty was put to the ultimate test on the rugged, sun-scorched cliffs of the Gallipoli Peninsula. The high-level strategy behind the attack was to knock the Ottoman Empire out of the war by seizing the narrow Dardanelles strait, but the reality on the ground was a disaster of planning and geography. The Australian and New Zealand forces, famously known as the ANZACs, were landed on the wrong beaches and found themselves trapped under the guns of a determined Ottoman defense. As the months dragged on in the heat and the dust, the casualty lists grew longer and longer. Back in the big cities of the Dominions, the initial excitement turned into a heavy, national grief. This was the moment the relationship with Britain began to change. The people of the colonies began to realize that their lives were being spent by British generals who were often disconnected from the reality of the front lines.

The political legacy of 1915 was a shift in the very soul of these nations. While they remained loyal to the empire, the shared tragedy of Gallipoli for the ANZACs and the brutal battles in France for the Canadians created a new kind of national pride. They began to realize that they were not just "British people living overseas," but something new and distinct. They had their own way of speaking, their own way of leading, and their own incredible resilience. The war, which was supposed to protect the old empire, was actually planting the seeds of independence. By the time the survivors of 1915 were moved to other fronts, the world had learned that the "colonials" were among the most effective fighting forces on the planet, and the young nations they represented would never be the same again.

7. Verdun and the Somme: The Year of Attrition

As the calendar turned to 1916, the war rooms of Europe were filled with a new and chilling kind of mathematics. The generals and politicians realized that the defensive lines were so strong that a traditional victory might be impossible. Instead of looking for a way around the enemy, the German high command decided to lean into the horror. They developed a strategy of pure attrition, designed not to capture land, but to destroy the enemy's soul. They chose the ancient, symbolic fortress city of Verdun as their target. They knew the French people viewed Verdun as a sacred symbol of their national pride, and that the French army would be forced to defend it at any cost. The goal was to create a giant "meat grinder" where they could simply bleed the French army until it had no men left to fight.

For nearly ten months, the maps of northern France remained frozen while the landscape around Verdun was transformed into a moonscape of craters and ash. The scale of the artillery fire was unlike anything humanity had ever seen, with millions of shells being fired into a tiny area of land. The high-level politics of this battle were incredibly intense. The French government made it clear to their generals that losing Verdun was not an option, as it would cause the entire country's morale to collapse. This forced the French to rotate almost their entire army through that single, terrifying sector. The battle became a national obsession, a test of which society was more willing to sacrifice its children for a few square miles of ruined earth.

To take the pressure off the gasping French army at Verdun, the British launched their own massive offensive further north, near a river called the Somme. This was the moment the world saw the true cost of the "Total War" that had been building since 1914. The British government had spent over a year preparing for this attack, building up a massive force of millions of volunteers. In the planning rooms in London, there was a hope that this would be the "Big Push" that would finally end the war. But when the attack began in the summer of 1916, it resulted in the bloodiest day in the history of the British military. The high-level reports coming back to the capital were so shocking that they were initially kept secret from the public to prevent a total panic.

The year 1916 changed the very atmosphere of the war. The "Great Rush" and the excitement of the early days were replaced by a heavy, silent endurance. In the big cities like London, Paris, and Berlin, the casualty lists were no longer just names in a newspaper; they were a presence in every home and every street. The politics of the war shifted toward a grim, industrial determination. Governments realized that they were now in a race to see which nation would break from the inside first. The war was no longer about grand maneuvers or heroic charges; it was a cold, mathematical contest of industrial production and human sacrifice. As the winter of 1916 approached, the leaders of the world were looking at a map that had barely moved, even though millions of lives had been spent to change it.

8. Conscription, Industry, and the Strain of Total War

By the middle of 1916, the political landscape in London and Paris was undergoing a massive shift as the true scale of the industrial slaughter became impossible to hide. The British government, which had started the war with a small, professional army, was now forced to confront the reality that a conflict of this size could only be sustained by the entire nation. This led to one of the most significant political decisions of the war: the introduction of conscription. For the first time in history, the British state claimed the power to force its citizens into military service. This move sparked intense debate in the halls of Parliament and in the streets of the big cities, as it challenged the very idea of individual liberty that Britain claimed to be fighting for.

The mood in the capital cities was also changing as the "Total War" began to hit the kitchen tables of ordinary families. In London, the government created a new Ministry of Munitions to take control of the country's factories, turning them into giant workshops for the front. Women flooded into the workforce to replace the men who had been sent to the Somme, working long hours in dangerous conditions to fill the endless demand for shells and explosives. This was a social revolution happening in the middle of a global catastrophe. The sight of women in trousers and overalls, doing jobs that had previously been reserved for men, was a sign that the old world was disappearing forever. The politics of the home front were now just as vital as the tactics of the generals, as the leaders realized that they had to keep the workers fed, housed, and motivated to prevent a total collapse of society.

In Paris, the atmosphere was even more strained. Because the war was being fought on French soil, the nation felt like it was being slowly consumed by a giant, hungry beast. The government had to manage the millions of refugees who had fled the occupied north, while also trying to keep the economy from falling apart. The "Sacred Union" of political parties that had formed at the start of the war was beginning to show cracks, as the mounting losses at Verdun led to finger-pointing and accusations of incompetence. The French leaders were walking a tightrope, trying to maintain the public's will to fight while the country's young men were being fed into the "meat grinder" by the hundreds of thousands.

By the end of 1916, the "Bird's Eye View" of the Allied powers showed a world that was being pushed to its absolute limit. The high-level coordination between Britain and France was becoming more formal, with the leaders meeting regularly to try and sync their strategies. They were no longer just two countries fighting the same enemy; they were becoming a single, massive war machine. But beneath the surface of this unified front, there was a growing sense of exhaustion and a realization that the old ways of governing and fighting were no longer enough. The war was forcing a total reorganization of human society, and the people in the big cities were beginning to wonder if the world would ever return to the peace they had known before the summer of 1914.

9. Jutland, Blockade, and the War at Sea

While the armies were locked in the mud of the Western Front, a different kind of war was being fought on the cold, grey waters of the North Sea. For decades, Britain and Germany had been locked in a massive arms race to build the most powerful navy in the world. Britain, as an island nation, relied on the sea for its very survival, while Germany saw a powerful fleet as the key to becoming a true global superpower. By 1916, these two giant forces finally met in the largest naval clash in history, the Battle of Jutland. On a bird's-eye map of the ocean, it looked like a choreographed dance of steel, with hundreds of ships and thousands of heavy guns firing across miles of open water. Although the battle was a chaotic and bloody mess that didn't result in a clear, crushing victory for either side, its political consequences were enormous.

The result of the battle confirmed a terrifying reality for Germany. Despite their incredible technology and bravery, they could not break the British naval blockade. This blockade was a silent but deadly weapon that was slowly strangling the German Empire. By stopping almost all ships from reaching German ports, Britain was cutting off the flow of food, fertilizer, and raw materials that the country needed to survive. In the big cities like Berlin and Vienna, the "Total War" was no longer just about soldiers on a map; it was about the empty shelves in the grocery stores. The German people were being forced to eat "ersatz" or substitute foods made of sawdust and dried turnips, and the health of the civilian population was beginning to decline rapidly.

The politics of the blockade were incredibly controversial. The German leaders argued that it was a crime to starve millions of innocent civilians, and they used this as a justification to launch their own desperate counter-attack at sea. They decided to use their U-boats to sink any ship, even those from neutral countries like the United States, that tried to bring supplies to Britain. This "unrestricted submarine warfare" was a massive political gamble. The German high command knew it might bring the United States into the war, but they were so desperate to break the British blockade that they were willing to take the risk. They hoped they could starve Britain into surrender before the Americans could even get their boots on.

By the end of 1916, the war at sea had turned the entire Atlantic Ocean into a battlefield. The high-level strategy was no longer just about sinking warships; it was about the survival of entire populations. The British were racing to build more merchant ships and find new ways to hunt submarines, while the Germans were racing to sink them. This was a cold, mathematical struggle of logistics and endurance. The world was witnessing a new kind of conflict where the hunger of a child in Berlin was directly connected to the path of a torpedo in the middle of the ocean. The blockade was a slow-motion catastrophe that was hollowing out the Central Powers from the inside, forcing their leaders toward even more radical and dangerous decisions in the year to come.

10. The Russian Revolution and the Collapse of the Eastern Front

As 1917 began, the most significant political earthquake of the war occurred in the East, where the massive Russian Empire finally reached its breaking point. For three years, the Russian people had endured unimaginable hardship. Their armies had suffered millions of casualties, and the country's economy was in total ruins. In the grand palaces of Petrograd, the Tsar and his advisors were increasingly disconnected from the reality of the streets, where the lack of bread and fuel had turned frustration into a boiling rage. The high-level view of Russia showed a nation that was no longer a functioning empire but a hollow shell, held together only by habit and fear. In March, that shell finally shattered.

The revolution began not with a grand military plan, but with thousands of hungry women and workers flooding into the streets to demand food. When the soldiers were ordered to fire on the crowds, they refused and instead joined the protesters. Within days, the Tsar was forced to give up his throne, ending centuries of imperial rule. This was a moment of incredible political chaos that changed the entire map of the war. At first, the new government tried to keep Russia in the fight, but the spirit of the army was gone. The soldiers began to walk away from the trenches by the thousands, heading back to their villages to take part in the redistribution of land. The Eastern Front, which had tied down half of the German army for years, was effectively disappearing.

The German leaders saw this as a golden opportunity and made a daring political move to ensure Russia's total collapse. They helped a radical revolutionary named Vladimir Lenin return to Russia from his exile in Switzerland, hoping he would stir up even more trouble. The plan worked perfectly. By the end of the year, Lenin's group, the Bolsheviks, seized power and immediately asked for a ceasefire. The Treaty of Brest-Litovsk, which followed, was a total surrender. Russia gave up vast amounts of land, including what is now Ukraine, Poland, and the Baltic states. For Germany, this was the ultimate strategic victory. They could now take their entire Eastern army and move it to the West for one final, crushing blow against Britain and France.

The collapse of Russia sent a wave of terror through the Allied capitals. In London and Paris, the leaders realized that they were about to face the full, undivided weight of the German military machine. The politics of the war had shifted from a struggle of two fronts to a desperate race for survival on one. But the revolution in Russia also sent a different kind of shockwave across the world. It was the first time a major power had been completely destroyed by the internal pressure of the war. It served as a chilling warning to every other government that there was a limit to how much a population could sacrifice before they would turn on their own leaders. The map of the East was being redrawn in the fires of revolution, and the world was watching to see if the same flames would spread to the rest of Europe.

11. The United States Enters the War

While the Russian Empire was collapsing in the East, a different kind of power was rising in the West. For the first three years of the war, the United States had maintained a careful and profitable neutrality. The American President, Woodrow Wilson, had even won re-election on the slogan that he had kept the country out of the war. However, the high-level politics of the conflict were making it increasingly impossible for America to stay on the sidelines. The German decision to resume unrestricted submarine warfare meant that American ships were being sunk and American lives were being lost. To the people in Washington, this was no longer just a European quarrel; it was an attack on the freedom of the seas and the rights of all neutral nations.

The final straw for the American government was a secret message known as the Zimmerman Telegram. In a desperate attempt to keep the United States busy at home, Germany had sent a coded proposal to Mexico, offering to help them reclaim lost territories like Texas and Arizona if they would attack the Americans. When the British intelligence services intercepted this message and shared it with the United States, the political mood in the country shifted overnight. The idea that a foreign power was trying to stir up a war on the American border was a step too far. In April 1917, the United States formally declared war on Germany, a decision that fundamentally changed the math of the global conflict.

The entry of the United States was a massive psychological and industrial boost for the exhausted Allies. While the British and French were running out of money and men, the Americans had a nearly limitless supply of both. The high-level view of the Atlantic showed a bridge of steel beginning to form, as thousands of troop ships and supply vessels started to move toward the ports of France. This wasn't just about soldiers; it was about the vast industrial power of the American Midwest, the oil of Texas, and the financial strength of Wall Street. The war had become a race against time. The German leaders knew that they had to win the war with their newly freed Eastern armies before the full weight of the American "crusade" could land in Europe.

By the end of 1917, the world was locked in a frantic, high-stakes competition. In the war rooms of Berlin, the generals were working day and night on a plan for one final, massive offensive. They knew that every day that passed brought more Americans to the front lines. In London and Paris, the leaders were doing everything they could to hold on, praying that their tired armies could survive one last German storm. The politics of the war had reached a fever pitch, as the conflict was now a battle between the old empires of Europe and the rising democratic power of the New World. The stage was set for the final, decisive year of the war, where the fate of the century would be decided by which side could move their resources across the map the fastest.

12. Germany's Last Great Offensive in 1918

As the spring of 1918 arrived, the German high command launched the most ambitious and desperate military operation of the entire war. With the Russian front closed, they had managed to move nearly fifty divisions of veteran soldiers to the West, giving them a temporary numerical advantage that they hadn't enjoyed since the very first weeks of 1914. The German leader, General Ludendorff, knew that this was the final window of opportunity. The bird's-eye view of the Western Front showed a massive concentration of German power aimed directly at the junction where the British and French armies met. The goal was to punch a hole through the Allied lines, drive the British into the sea, and capture Paris before the American army was large enough to intervene.

The offensive, which began in March, was a tactical masterclass that initially shattered the long-standing stalemate. Using new methods of surprise and speed, the German forces broke through the trench lines that had been frozen for years. On the maps in the Allied headquarters, the red lines of the German advance began to move with terrifying speed, swallowing up territory that had been fought over for years in just a few days. The political atmosphere in London and Paris reached a point of near-panic. The threat was so great that the Allies finally agreed to do something they had resisted for years: they appointed a single supreme commander, the French General Foch, to coordinate all their forces. This was a major political turning point, as it allowed the Allies to finally act as a unified machine rather than a collection of separate national armies.

Despite their initial success, the German gamble began to fail because of the very "Total War" conditions they had helped create. As their soldiers advanced, they outran their supply lines and their heavy guns. The German troops, who had been living on starvation rations for years due to the naval blockade, were shocked to find Allied supply depots filled with white bread, chocolate, and fine wine. Many soldiers stopped to loot these supplies instead of continuing the attack, a sign that the discipline of the German army was beginning to erode under the weight of years of deprivation. Meanwhile, the first large groups of American soldiers were finally entering the lines, providing a fresh and enthusiastic wall of defense that the exhausted Germans simply couldn't break.

By the early summer of 1918, the German offensive had ground to a halt. They had gained a lot of ground on the map, but they had failed to achieve a decisive victory. More importantly, they had lost their best, most experienced soldiers in the process. The high-level view of the war now showed a German army that was overextended and physically spent, facing an Allied force that was growing stronger and more unified every day. The gamble had failed, and the initiative had passed permanently to the Allies. The German leaders realized with a sinking heart that they had thrown their last pair of dice and come up short. The war was no longer a contest that Germany could win; it was now a question of how long they could hold on before the inevitable collapse.

13. The Hundred Days Offensive and the Collapse of the Central Powers

By the summer of 1918, the momentum of the war had shifted in a way that felt like a physical weight lifting off the Allied powers. Sensing that the German army was finally at its breaking point, General Foch launched what would become known as the Hundred Days Offensive. This was not just one single battle, but a series of coordinated strikes across the entire Western Front that hit the German lines like a succession of hammer blows. On the high-level maps in the Allied war rooms, the static lines that had defined the conflict for four years were suddenly in constant, fluid motion. The Allies were now using their industrial superiority to its full effect, coordinating their infantry with hundreds of tanks and thousands of aircraft in a way that the exhausted German forces simply could not match.

As the German army was pushed back, the political foundations of the Central Powers began to crumble with stunning speed. In the big cities of Germany and Austria-Hungary, the years of starvation and loss had finally pushed the people beyond their limits. The high-level view of these empires showed a total internal collapse. In Austria-Hungary, the different ethnic groups (the Czechs, the Poles, the South Slavs) were all declaring their independence, effectively dismantling the empire from within. In Germany, the news of the military retreat triggered a wave of strikes and mutinies. The sailors in the German fleet, ordered to sail out for one last suicidal battle, refused to obey, sparking a revolution that spread to the factories and the streets of Berlin.

The politics of the war had reached their final, desperate stage. The German leaders realized that they were no longer fighting for victory, but to prevent a total social and political disintegration of their country. They began to send frantic messages to the American President, hoping to negotiate a peace based on his idealistic promises of a fair settlement. But the Allied leaders in London and Paris, who had sacrificed so much, were in no mood for a gentle peace. They demanded a total military surrender. The German Kaiser was forced to give up his throne and flee into exile, ending the German Empire that had been born in the fires of a previous war forty-seven years earlier.

By early November 1918, the maps showed the Central Powers in total retreat on every front. Bulgaria, the Ottoman Empire, and Austria-Hungary had all signed separate agreements to stop fighting, leaving Germany completely alone. The world was witnessing the simultaneous collapse of three of the most powerful empires in history. The high-level view was one of total upheaval, as the old order of kings and emperors was being swept away by a tide of military defeat and internal revolution. The war that had begun with such excitement and grand plans was ending in a chaotic, desperate scramble to stop the violence before it consumed what was left of European civilization.

14. The Armistice of 11 November 1918

The end of World War I did not arrive with a final, climactic battle, but with a quiet meeting in a railway carriage hidden deep within the cold, misty woods of the Forest of Compiègne. In the early morning hours of November 11, 1918, the representatives of a broken German Empire sat across from the Allied commanders to sign a document that would finally stop the slaughter. It is important to understand that what they signed was not a peace treaty, but an armistice. In the high-level language of international politics, a peace treaty is a permanent agreement that settles all the reasons why a war started in the first place. An armistice, however, is simply a formal agreement to stop the fighting; a massive, global "time-out." The German leaders were so terrified of a total revolution at home and a complete military collapse at the front that they needed the guns to stop immediately, even if it meant accepting humiliating terms.

The timing of this ceasefire was chosen with a sense of poetic drama that would be remembered for centuries. It was decided that the guns would fall silent at exactly eleven o'clock in the morning, the eleventh hour of the eleventh day of the eleventh month. This was a bird's-eye decision made by the top generals to ensure that the news had enough time to travel across the hundreds of miles of front lines. But for the men in the mud, those final six hours between the signing at 5:00 a.m. and the actual ceasefire at 11:00 a.m. were a surreal and tragic experience. Because the war was still technically "on," some commanders continued to order attacks, and artillery continued to fire right up until the final second. Thousands of men were killed or wounded on that final morning, their lives spent for ground that would be surrendered just a few hours later.

When the clock finally struck eleven, a strange and haunting silence swept across the world. For more than fifteen hundred days, the air in Europe had been filled with the constant, low-frequency rumble of heavy guns and the sharp crack of rifles. Suddenly, there was nothing but the sound of the wind and the occasional bird. On the maps in the war rooms, the red and blue lines that had pulsed and bled for years simply stopped moving. In the big cities like London, Paris, and New York, the news triggered a wave of celebration so intense it was described as a kind of madness. People danced in the streets, church bells rang out for hours, and total strangers embraced. But in the trenches, the mood was often one of numb disbelief. Many soldiers simply sat down where they were, unable to process that the world they had known, a world of constant death and fear, was actually over.

The "Long Shadow" of this moment would stretch far into the future. Because the war ended with an armistice rather than a total invasion of Germany, a dangerous political myth began to grow in the minds of the defeated. Many Germans felt that their army hadn't actually been beaten on the battlefield, but had been "stabbed in the back" by the politicians and revolutionaries at home. This sense of bitterness and unfinished business would eventually poison the politics of the next twenty years. Meanwhile, the four-year struggle had dismantled the very foundations of the old world. Four massive empires had vanished, and the maps were being redrawn by diplomats in Paris who were trying to build a new world out of the ruins of the old. World War I had ended, but it had left behind a globe that was fragile, grieving, and deeply unsettled. A world that was no longer at war, but was not yet truly at peace.

TWO

Making a Soldier

At the start of the war, the rush to join the military was driven by a mix of excitement, social pressure, and a deep sense of duty. Ordinary men who had spent their lives in quiet offices or on family farms suddenly found themselves standing in long lines to sign their names to the cause. This chapter looks at the reality of those early days, from the clever ways people were encouraged to volunteer to the first, often difficult steps of military training. It was a massive shift that turned millions of civilians into a new kind of army, changing their lives and their communities forever.

15. The Medical Exam That Decided Who Went to War

Before a man ever reached the trenches, he first had to pass through the army's medical board, a process far stricter and more methodical than most recruits expected. The exam wasn't just a quick glance. It was designed to filter out anyone who might break down under weeks of marching, digging, or carrying heavy loads. Men lined up half-naked in cold town halls or depots while doctors worked down the row like mechanics inspecting parts. Height and weight were recorded. Chests were measured during deep breaths to check lung capacity, because weak lungs meant poor endurance or higher risk of pneumonia. Hearts were listened to for murmurs or irregular rhythms, since long marches and battlefield stress could trigger collapse. Pulse rate was taken at rest to spot nervous or unhealthy candidates. Eyesight was tested against charts across the room, hearing checked with whispered commands, teeth inspected because untreated infections could disable a soldier in days. Even feet were closely examined. Flat feet were a common reason for rejection, not because they looked unusual, but because the army knew men with collapsed arches developed crippling pain and blisters after marching 10–20 miles (16–32 km) a day under load. A soldier who couldn't walk couldn't fight.

Recruits were graded into categories: fully fit for front-line duty, fit only for labor or support roles, or unfit entirely. Roughly a third failed their first exam. Knowing this, some desperate men tried to manipulate the results. They starved themselves to weigh less, sprinted in place to spike their heart rate, pretended not to hear instructions, memorized eye charts incorrectly, or complained loudly of back pain and "weak nerves." A few stuffed cotton in their ears or deliberately limped. Most attempts failed, but the fact that so many tried shows how terrifying the alternative seemed.

16. Training Camp: Turning Recruits Into Soldiers

Soldiers who passed their medicals were issued rough wool uniforms, heavy boots, rifles, and kit, then sent almost immediately to training camps, vast muddy cities of tents and wooden huts that could hold tens of thousands of recruits at once. Many had never been away from home before, yet within days they found themselves living shoulder to shoulder with strangers in crowded barracks that smelled of damp canvas, boot polish, and coal smoke. Life began before sunrise. Bugles (a small brass wind instrument used to signal commands in the army, its loud, clear notes carried across camps and battlefields to wake soldiers, start drills, announce meals, or sound alarms when shouted voices couldn't be heard) blasted around 5:00 a.m., dragging everyone from their blankets. Within minutes men stood outside for roll call, boots half-laced, breath fogging in the cold.

Days followed a relentless rhythm built around repetition and exhaustion. Route marches of 8–12 miles (13–19 km) were routine, and longer marches of 15–20 miles (24–32 km) were common to harden legs and feet. All of it was done carrying a full kit weighing 60–70 pounds (27–32 kilograms), sometimes more with extra ammunition. Shoulders blistered. Hips bruised. Straps cut into skin. Recruits quickly learned how physically heavy war really was.

Hours were spent drilling with rifles until every movement became automatic: load, aim, fire, cycle the bolt, fire again. Instructors demanded speed and rhythm, sometimes timing volleys with a stopwatch, pushing men to fire fifteen or more aimed rounds a minute until their shoulders throbbed and fingers cramped. Bayonet practice was even more brutal and personal. Recruits charged rows of straw-filled dummies while sergeants screamed inches from their faces to "thrust, twist, withdraw," teaching them not only how to stab but how to overcome hesitation. The goal was to remove fear and replace it with instinct. Some camps built mock trenches where men leapt in and out while lunging at targets, shouting battle cries to build aggression.

Grenade training took place in deep sandbagged pits where live explosives were handled under supervision. Recruits practiced pulling pins, counting seconds, and throwing fast before the fuse burned down. Mistakes could be fatal, and accidents occasionally injured or killed trainees, a grim reminder that even preparation was dangerous. Gas-mask drills were sudden and frightening. Without warning, whistles blew and instructors released tear gas or chlorine simulants. Men had only seconds to fit their masks. Anyone too slow felt their eyes burn and lungs seize, sometimes collapsing coughing in the dirt while others scrambled to help. The lesson was simple: hesitation meant death.

Entire afternoons were devoted to trench practice. Soldiers dug full-scale trenches by hand with entrenching tools, reinforced them with sandbags and duckboards, built fire steps and parapets, and learned drainage so the trench wouldn't flood. Then they moved through the maze under simulated fire, hauling ammunition, carrying stretchers, or rushing messages from one end to the other. Often, after hours of exhausting labor, they filled the trenches back in, only to dig them again the next day, repeating the cycle purely to build strength and muscle memory.

Lectures filled whatever time remained. Men were taught map reading, signaling with flags and lamps, first aid for bleeding wounds, how to recognize gas clouds, how to clean rifles properly, trench etiquette, disease prevention, and even how to write letters that wouldn't reveal military secrets. Veterans freshly returned from the front sometimes spoke bluntly about what to expect: mud, lice, fear, and the constant thunder of artillery.

Most instructors were professional sergeants or hardened veterans rotated back from the front, men already shaped by combat and impatient with mistakes. Discipline was harsh by design. The smallest error could mean punishment. Late for parade brought extra drill. Dirty boots meant confinement. Talking back cost pay. "Fatigue duty" meant endless chores like hauling water or digging pits after everyone else rested. "Pack punishment" forced a man to march for hours carrying full gear. Some were given Field Punishment No. 1, strapped upright to a post or wheel for hours under guard, exposed to wind and rain. It wasn't meant to injure, only to humiliate and deter. The message was clear: obedience had to be instant.

Training length depended on the war's urgency. Early in 1914–15, recruits might spend three to six months preparing. By 1917–18, as casualties soared, some men were rushed through in six to eight weeks or less, arriving at the front barely trained.

17. Specialist Roles and the Journey to the Front

After basic training, recruits were no longer treated as one mass of identical men. Officers began sorting them by ability, temperament, and simple physical build, quietly deciding who might survive longest in each role. Most became ordinary infantry riflemen, the backbone of every army, expected to march, dig, shoot, and hold the line under any condition. Better shots or calmer personalities were often chosen as scouts or snipers, men who worked in pairs, crawling ahead of the trenches to observe enemy movement or waiting motionless for hours behind a scope. Larger, stronger men were assigned to machine-gun crews, hauling heavy weapons and thousands of rounds of ammunition, or to stretcher-bearer teams who carried wounded soldiers through mud and shellfire, often unarmed and exposed. Engineers became sappers or tunnel diggers, some of the most claustrophobic and dangerous jobs in the war, burrowing underground for weeks to plant explosives beneath enemy trenches while listening for enemy miners doing the same. Others trained as signalers laying telephone wire, runners carrying messages across open ground, medics treating the wounded under fire, artillery gunners loading massive shells, drivers operating trucks and ambulances, or pigeon handlers caring for the birds that sometimes served as the only reliable communication during battle. Officers either came from separate academies or were promoted from the ranks after extra leadership courses, suddenly responsible for the lives of dozens of men they had once stood beside. A few volunteers stepped forward for especially dangerous specialties like flamethrower units or bombing squads, roles with frightening casualty rates but critical tasks in assaults.

Once assigned, recruits were grouped into companies and battalions that often stayed together for the rest of the war. Then came the journey to the front. Trains rattled them toward coastal ports, kit bags piled high, rifles stacked in corners. Ships carried them across the Channel in crowded holds smelling of oil and seasickness. Bands sometimes played and civilians waved flags, cheering as if sending men to an adventure rather than a slaughter. Many soldiers still imagined glory at this stage, postcards and photographs tucked into their pockets.

Yet even after reaching France or Belgium, they did not go straight into battle. New arrivals usually spent days or weeks in reserve or base camps behind the lines, drilling again, unloading supplies, filling sandbags, and learning practical trench habits from veterans who spoke quietly and without drama about what to expect: how to keep your head down, how to sleep through shellfire, how to spot gas, how to survive. It was called "seasoning," a final adjustment period meant to toughen nerves before exposure to the front.

18. The Heavy Load Every Soldier Carried

Before a soldier ever fired a shot, he first had to lift the war onto his back. In "full marching order," a British or Commonwealth infantryman carried far more than just a rifle. Slung over one shoulder was his rifle and bayonet, along with 120–150 rounds, roughly 8–10 pounds (3–4 kilograms) of bullets of ammunition packed into bandoliers and pouches that thumped against his chest as he walked. Around his neck hung a water bottle and a small canvas bag holding his gas mask, a constant reminder that poison gas could come without warning. Strapped to his belt was an entrenching tool, a short-handled shovel used to dig trenches, graves, or cover in seconds. Tied to his pack sat a mess tin, a battered metal container that served as his entire kitchen, used to boil tea, heat stew, or eat whatever rations he could get.

On his back he carried spare socks and underwear, soap, a razor, toothbrush, sewing kit, knife, letters from home, photographs, cigarettes or tobacco, matches, and any small comforts that made life feel human. Rolled tightly on top was his greatcoat, a thick wool overcoat that doubled as winter jacket, blanket, pillow, and sometimes even a mattress. Dry, it was heavy; soaked with rain and mud, it could feel like carrying another person. Add one or two days of hard rations (biscuits, tinned meat, jam, tea, sugar), and the weight kept climbing. Before attacks, extra gear piled on: several Mills bombs, the iron "pineapple" grenades that weighed nearly 1.5 pounds (0.7 kilograms) each, often two to four as standard and sometimes six or more stuffed into pockets, plus extra ammunition or tools.

Altogether, the load typically reached 60–70 pounds (27–32 kilograms), and sometimes more than 80 pounds (36+ kilograms), roughly the weight of a large suitcase or a small child. Soldiers didn't wear it every minute in the trenches, but whenever rotating between lines, marching to the front, or preparing for battle, everything went on at once. Men climbed ladders out of trenches, crawled under wire, and slogged through knee-deep mud with that weight dragging at their shoulders. Straps rubbed skin raw, backs ached constantly, and boots sank deep into the ground with every step. By the time they reached the fight, many were already exhausted. Some quietly discarded gear along the way just to move faster. The burden also explained why many experimental ideas, like steel body armor or wheeled shields, failed immediately: most soldiers were already carrying as much as the human body could endure.

19. Fighting for Pennies at the Front

Many soldiers carried sixty or seventy pounds of gear, slept in mud, and faced artillery every day, yet were paid barely more than pocket change. A regular British private earned just 1 shilling a day. Adjusted for modern value, that equals roughly $8–$10 USD per day in today's money, about the price of a sandwich and coffee. A full week at the front brought in only $55–$65, and a month's pay barely reached $250. From that small amount, deductions were sometimes taken for damaged equipment or small comforts, leaving even less. Corporals and sergeants earned only slightly more, while officers paid for many of their own uniforms and expenses out of pocket. German and French infantry wages were similarly tiny. Many soldiers joked that the cigarettes or chocolate in a parcel from home were worth more than their official pay. In reality, money mattered little at the front, there was almost nothing to spend it on, but the numbers reveal something striking. Millions of young men risked their lives daily for what would now amount to minimum wage.

20. From Bright Uniforms to Mud-Colored War

Before World War I, soldiers often marched into battle in bright colors meant to impress rather than hide, but the trenches quickly erased any trace of parade-ground style. By 1915, nearly every army had switched to dull, muddy tones designed to blend into earth and smoke. British and Commonwealth troops wore khaki wool tunics and trousers, the French abandoned their famous blue coats and red trousers for "horizon blue," and German soldiers adopted field-grey uniforms that disappeared easily against mud and concrete. From a distance, and especially after a few days in the trenches, everyone looked roughly the same: brown, grey, and filthy. Rain, clay, and smoke quickly coated uniforms until color barely mattered.

The clothing itself was heavy and uncomfortable. Thick wool was chosen for warmth and durability, but when soaked by rain it absorbed water like a sponge, doubling in weight and drying slowly in the cold. Tunics scratched, seams rubbed skin raw, and lice thrived in the fabric. Around their lower legs, many British troops wrapped long cloth strips called puttees to support their ankles and keep mud out of their boots, though these often trapped moisture instead. Boots were stiff leather with iron hobnails hammered into the soles for grip, tough but slippery on duckboards and loud on hard ground. Steel helmets gradually replaced soft caps after the first year of the war, protecting men from falling shrapnel and debris rather than direct bullets. Each army developed its own shape, the shallow British Brodie, the deep German Stahlhelm, the French Adrian, giving the front lines a forest of strange metal silhouettes bobbing above the trenches.

Despite these differences, identity blurred quickly. In fog, smoke, or darkness, uniforms lost all meaning and soldiers fired at movement rather than color. A man crawling through mud at night looked like any other shadow. By the end of a week in the trenches, coats were torn, knees patched, and everything stained the same dull brown. The carefully issued uniform became something more primitive: just another layer between a soldier and the cold, the lice, and the war.

21. Killed by Their Own Side

Not every shell that killed a soldier came from the enemy. In the chaos of trench warfare, thousands of men were wounded or killed by their own side, a grim reality that soldiers bluntly called "short rounds" or simply "our own guns," because the modern phrase "friendly fire" didn't yet exist. Artillery batteries often fired from miles away using rough maps and smoke-obscured targets, and even small errors in range could drop shells directly onto friendly trenches. During attacks, creeping barrages were meant to land just ahead of advancing infantry and slowly move forward, but if the timing was wrong or the guns fired too short, explosions tore into the very men they were supposed to protect. At night or in fog, units sometimes fired on their own patrols, mistaking movement for the enemy. Signal flares were misread, coordinates confused, and messages lost when runners were killed. Gas attacks occasionally drifted back with the wind, choking the troops who released it. Even aircraft bombed the wrong lines.

Exact numbers are impossible to calculate, but historians estimate that friendly fire accounted for a significant percentage of battlefield casualties, in some battles reaching 5–10 percent or more. Soldiers grew grimly accustomed to it. Diaries mention the bitter irony of surviving enemy fire only to be shelled by their own artillery minutes later.

22. The Rifles That Kept Soldiers Alive

By the time a soldier climbed onto the fire step and raised his rifle over the parapet, the weapon in his hands might determine whether he lived through the next ten seconds or not. Although all sides carried bolt-action rifles that looked similar from a distance, their performance varied dramatically. British troops used the Short Magazine Lee–Enfield (SMLE), a rugged .303 rifle with a large 10-round magazine and an unusually smooth, fast bolt. It could be reloaded with two 5-round stripper clips in just a few seconds, and trained infantry were expected to fire 15–25 aimed shots per minute. Some could fire even faster. During training, British soldiers practiced the famous "Mad Minute," trying to hit a target fifteen times at 300 yards (275 meters) in sixty seconds. Skilled marksmen sometimes doubled that, firing so rapidly that Germans occasionally mistook concentrated rifle fire for machine guns.

German soldiers carried the Mauser Gewehr 98, one of the strongest and most accurate rifles of the war. It fired a powerful 7.92 mm cartridge and had a long barrel that made it excellent at distance shooting. But it held only 5 rounds, and the longer, stiffer bolt meant reloads were slightly slower. A typical German infantryman managed around 10–15 aimed shots per minute. The rifle was famously reliable and precise, which made it a favorite with snipers, but in the chaos of close trench fighting, its smaller magazine could feel limiting.

French troops began the war with the outdated Lebel 1886, which loaded cartridges one by one into a tube magazine under the barrel. Topping it off could take twenty or thirty seconds, an eternity under fire. Later they replaced it with the Berthier rifle, which used 3- or 5-round clips and loaded much faster, though still not as quickly as the Lee–Enfield. Across the front, soldiers quickly learned that rate of fire mattered just as much as accuracy when an enemy charge appeared through the smoke.

A rifle was only part of the load. Ammunition came in bandoliers and pouches, usually 120–150 rounds carried as standard issue, sometimes more before attacks. Bayonets fixed to the muzzle turned the gun into a spear for close quarters. Mud, rain, and trench grit constantly jammed actions, so men cleaned and oiled their rifles obsessively, sometimes sleeping with them tucked under their coats to keep rust away. A jam at the wrong moment could mean death.

In practice, these differences shaped the battlefield. British units could unleash rapid, sustained volleys that pinned attackers down. German rifles excelled at deliberate, accurate fire from cover. French troops compensated with grenades and aggressive tactics to make up for slower reloads. To the soldiers themselves, the debate was simple and personal. The best rifle wasn't the most elegant or powerful. It was the one that could be reloaded fastest, fired the most times, and still worked when soaked in mud at dawn, because in the trenches, a few extra rounds and a few saved seconds could be the thin line between firing back or never firing again.

23. The Specialist Weapons That Controlled the Battlefield

Not every soldier in the trench fought as a simple rifleman. Some belonged to specialist teams whose weapons could shape entire battles. The most feared were machine-gun crews. Instead of a light rifle, they hauled heavy, water-cooled guns like the British Vickers, the German MG08, or the French Hotchkiss, mounted on sturdy tripods and fed by long fabric belts of ammunition. A single gun weighed around 30–40 pounds (14–18 kilograms), and with tripod, spare barrels, water cans, tools, and thousands of rounds, a full team's load could exceed 100 pounds (45 kilograms). It usually took four to six men to operate: one firing, one feeding the belt, one spotting targets, and others carrying ammunition and cooling water. Once set up, the gun could fire 450–600 rounds per minute, fast enough to sweep entire fields in seconds. The goal wasn't precision shooting but area denial, creating invisible walls of bullets that could cut down charging infantry or pin enemies in place. During major attacks, machine guns often accounted for more casualties than rifles or artillery, turning open ground into killing zones.

Alongside them were bombing squads, the close-quarters fighters of the trench system. Armed not just with rifles but with satchels of hand grenades, extra ammunition, and sometimes clubs or trench knives, these men specialized in clearing enemy trenches one corner at a time. A typical British "bomber" might carry 10–20 Mills bombs (each about 1.5 pounds / 0.7 kilograms), tucked into pockets or sandbags slung over the shoulder. In raids, they moved ahead of riflemen, lobbing grenades around bends or into dugouts before rushing forward through smoke and debris. Fighting was often at arm's length, chaotic and brutal. It was considered one of the most dangerous jobs in the war, requiring speed, strength, and nerves of steel. Casualties were high, but these squads were essential for breaking through trench lines where rifles alone couldn't reach.

Together, machine-gun teams and bombers formed the heavy muscle of the infantry, one dominating the battlefield at long range with relentless streams of fire, the other smashing through tight trench corners with explosions and shock. While the average soldier carried one rifle, these specialists carried the weapons that truly controlled the ground.

24. The Fragile Wires That Held the Front Together

Despite the scale of artillery and machine guns, most communication on the Western Front depended on something surprisingly fragile: thin copper telephone wires stretched across the ground. Radios were bulky, unreliable, and rarely used at the front, so armies relied on field telephones connected by miles of cable linking trenches, headquarters, artillery batteries, and observation posts. Signalers spent hours unspooling wire reels through mud, shell holes, and barbed wire, sometimes laying lines at night while bullets snapped overhead.

The problem was that these lines broke constantly. Shellfire shredded them. Tanks crushed them. Passing soldiers tripped over them. Rain and mud shorted them out. A single bombardment could cut every connection in minutes, leaving entire sectors suddenly silent. When that happened, small teams nicknamed "wire soldiers" or "linesmen" crawled out with repair kits, following the cable by hand across no man's land to find the break. They often worked under active fire, kneeling in mud to twist the ends back together while artillery continued to fall around them. It was one of the most dangerous jobs in the trenches, because the wire itself led straight toward command posts that the enemy was already targeting.

THREE

Life in the Trenches

For the millions of men who served on the Western Front, the war was not defined by grand movements on a map, but by the narrow, muddy world of the trenches. These deep ditches in the earth became the permanent home for an entire generation of soldiers, stretching for hundreds of miles across the landscape of Europe. Life in this underground world was a constant struggle against the environment as much as the enemy. This chapter looks at the daily reality of that existence, from the constant battle with mud and water to the strange and difficult conditions that soldiers had to endure just to survive from one day to the next.

25. The Dawn and Dusk Ritual of the Trenches

Trench life followed a strict daily rhythm built around the most dangerous hours of the day: dawn and dusk, when visibility was poor and surprise attacks were easiest. In the half-light of early morning or fading sunset, shadows were long, fog hung low, and it was difficult to tell whether movement in no man's land was a patrol or an advancing assault. Commanders knew many attacks began at these moments, so twice a day the entire line went on full alert for "stand-to." Often around 4:30 or 5:00 a.m. in summer and closer to 7:00 a.m. in winter, every soldier climbed onto the trench's "fire step," a narrow ledge built into the wall that allowed them to stand high enough to shoot over the parapet (the raised wall of packed earth and sandbags at the front of the trench that protected soldiers from enemy fire). Rifles were loaded, bayonets fixed, and men waited silently, scanning the mist for shapes or sounds. The same tense ritual repeated at sunset. Between those alerts, the day filled with repairs, cleaning weapons, hauling supplies, and "sentry duty," where individuals took turns standing watch for an hour or two at a time, peering over the trench while everyone else tried to rest. The routine created a strange contrast: hours of boredom and chores interrupted predictably by two daily moments when everyone expected the war to explode without warning.

26. When Weather Became a Weapon

Weather often proved as dangerous as the enemy, and mud became one of the most constant enemies of trench life. Heavy rain could fall for days without stopping, turning carefully dug trenches into brown canals of standing water. Walls collapsed, duckboards floated loose, and men sometimes sank calf-deep or even waist-deep when they stepped off the wooden walkways. Boots were sucked off by the mud, rifles clogged with grit, and supplies delayed because wagons and horses simply could not move forward. In winter, the same ground froze solid, coating sandbags and uniforms with frost and leaving fingers too numb to pull triggers easily. In summer, the mud baked into cracked earth that smelled of rot and decay. Soldiers often joked that they weren't fighting for land so much as drowning in it. Many veterans later said the mud, not the bullets, was what they remembered most.

27. The Disease That Rottted Soldiers' Feet

Constant moisture created one of the most feared non-combat injuries of the war: trench foot. Soldiers' boots were rarely dry, and many men stood for hours in cold water or mud that seeped through seams and soaked their socks day after day. Without circulation or warmth, feet first turned pale and numb, then swollen and blotchy, the skin softening and peeling like wet paper. Blisters formed, infections set in, and a sour, rotten smell often followed. In severe cases the flesh blackened and died, sometimes leading to gangrene and amputation. Commanders quickly learned that entire units could be crippled without a single shot fired, so soldiers were ordered to change socks frequently, rub their feet with whale oil (a thick waterproof grease made by boiling whale fat, cheap and widely available at the time), and stand on duckboards whenever possible to keep out of standing water. Inspections became routine, with officers checking feet the same way they checked rifles. Even so, thousands were evacuated each year with damaged feet, proof that the mud itself could be as dangerous as the enemy.

28. Sanitation, Smell, and Disease in the Trenches

Sanitation was another constant struggle, and the smell of the trenches became something many veterans said they could never forget. Toilets were usually nothing more than shallow slit trenches dug a short distance behind the line, sometimes screened with sandbags or scraps of canvas for privacy. Men balanced on wooden planks or simply crouched over the pit, which quickly filled and had to be covered with earth and replaced. In crowded sectors or during heavy fighting, proper facilities broke down entirely, forcing soldiers to use buckets or improvised containers that had to be emptied by hand. Flies gathered in thick swarms, spreading germs between waste, food, and living spaces. When the wind shifted, the odor of mud, smoke, sweat, rotting sandbags, and human waste drifted straight through the trenches, clinging to clothes and blankets. Combined with poor water and cramped conditions, these unsanitary setups helped spread diarrhea, dysentery, and stomach illnesses almost as reliably as enemy fire.

29. Rations in the Trenches

Food was issued with military precision and rarely changed. A typical British daily ration included about 1 pound (450 grams) of bread or hard biscuits, 12–16 ounces (340–450 grams) of meat when available, plus small portions of cheese or jam and, above all, tea. Fresh food almost never reached the front, so meals usually meant tinned stew, salted beef, or thick soup heated over tiny trench stoves. Sugar was rationed carefully and treated like treasure, often saved for tea rather than eaten outright. Anything from home (chocolate, butter, sausage, or a loaf of real soft bread) felt like a luxury beyond imagination. Soldiers quickly learned to eat whenever food appeared, because the next delivery might be delayed for days by mud, broken supply lines, or shellfire cutting the roads behind them.

30. The Drink That Held British Troops Together

Tea became almost sacred to British troops, less a simple drink than a daily ritual that structured life in the trenches. Whenever there was a pause in shelling, men immediately set about boiling water in dented metal mess tins or blackened kettles balanced over tiny fires made from scraps of wood, coal, or solid fuel tablets. The brew was strong black tea leaves carried in ration sacks, usually mixed with condensed milk and as much sugar as a soldier could spare. A mug marked the rhythm of the day: one at dawn after "stand-to," another after long marches or repair work, another before night sentry duty. In the cold, wet trenches, that hot sweetness cut through mud, smoke, and exhaustion better than any medicine.

The habit became so universal that it occasionally created problems. Small cooking fires sent thin columns of smoke into the air, and enemy observers sometimes spotted these "tea smokes" rising from the lines, revealing occupied positions. Officers repeatedly ordered men not to light fires during daylight, but the rules were widely ignored. Soldiers joked that they would sooner miss a meal than miss their tea. Commanders eventually realized that banning it hurt morale more than it helped security, so instead they adapted, issuing safer trench stoves, braziers (a small metal container filled with coals used as a portable stove or heater), and insulated water cans so hot water could be prepared more discreetly.

Over time, tea became shorthand for comfort itself. Men shared mugs during quiet moments, traded sugar for favors, and used tea breaks as excuses to talk, complain, or simply feel human again. Veterans later wrote that a single hot drink could steady nerves after bombardment better than any speech from an officer. The dependence grew so ingrained that British military planners eventually designed vehicles with built-in boiling equipment so crews could heat water without leaving cover.

31. The Postal System That Reached the Front

Letters and parcels from home became lifelines that connected the trenches to normal life, and armies built surprisingly efficient postal systems to keep them moving. At the height of the war, the scale was staggering, with an estimated 12 million letters delivered to the Western Front every single week, turning the military post into one of the largest logistical operations of the conflict. Soldiers could usually send letters for free, marking them 'On Active Service,' while the government covered the postage. They were handed to unit runners who carried sacks of mail back through the lines to field post offices, where trains and ships carried them across the Channel. A note written in France might reach England in as little as two or three days during quiet periods, though heavy fighting could stretch delivery to weeks. Parcels followed more slowly and unpredictably. Families packed tins of biscuits, chocolate, tea, tobacco, socks, scarves, or even small cakes, hoping the contents survived the journey. Some boxes arrived crushed, moldy, or raided along the way, but when one made it through intact, it felt like a holiday. Men often shared the contents with their whole dugout, turning a single bar of chocolate or a pair of dry socks into an event everyone remembered. In a world of mud and rations, a letter in familiar handwriting or a package smelling faintly of home could lift morale more than any order or speech.

32. When Private Messages Became Military Secrets

Every letter leaving the trenches passed through human censors before it ever reached home, and that meant officers physically reading thousands of private messages by hand. At the company or battalion level, junior officers or sergeants sat at rough tables with piles of envelopes, opening each one and scanning for anything that revealed locations, unit names, casualties, or upcoming plans. If a soldier wrote "We're near Ypres" or "we attack tomorrow," the censor simply struck the line through with ink, cut it out with scissors, or blacked it over entirely before stamping the page "Passed by Censor." The work was slow and tedious, sometimes hundreds of letters in a single evening, and many officers disliked the job, calling it punishment duty. Yet commanders insisted on it, knowing that one careless sentence intercepted by the enemy could expose an entire sector of the front. As a result, most letters home arrived with awkward gaps or missing lines, quiet reminders that even personal words were part of the war.

33. Smoking, Drinking, and Surviving the War

Tobacco and alcohol became two of the most common comforts in the trenches, woven so deeply into daily life that many soldiers later said the war had turned them into lifelong smokers and drinkers. Cigarettes were everywhere. Armies issued them in rations, families packed them into parcels, and they quickly became a form of currency traded for food, favors, or information. By some estimates, more than three-quarters of British troops smoked regularly, and countless young men who had never touched tobacco before the war picked up the habit simply to calm their nerves or pass the endless hours of waiting. A shared smoke meant conversation, warmth, and a brief moment of normalcy. Alcohol was treated more cautiously but still common. British soldiers sometimes received small rum rations before cold nights or attacks, French troops were often issued wine, and beer or spirits appeared more freely in rest areas behind the lines. Drinking dulled fear and helped men sleep, though drunkenness near the front was punished strictly. Stories later exaggerated the idea of soldiers seeking stronger highs, but in reality most relied on nothing more exotic than nicotine, strong tea, and occasional rum.

34. Games and Small Escapes in the Trenches

Long stretches of waiting filled far more hours than fighting, and soldiers quickly invented small rituals and games to keep boredom from becoming unbearable. Card games like poker, pontoon (blackjack), and brag were played on overturned ammunition crates or flattened ration boxes, with cigarettes, chocolate, or extra sugar used as makeshift currency instead of money. Dice rattled in mess tins, coins were flipped, and arguments over rules broke up the monotony of damp afternoons. In reserve areas behind the lines, men kicked footballs through muddy fields, staged impromptu boxing matches, or tested their strength in wrestling contests, cheering loudly for anyone who could momentarily forget the war.

Others filled the quiet hours more gently. Some carved chess sets or dominoes from scrap wood and shell crates, whittled pipes, or etched souvenirs from spent bullets. Newspapers and dog-eared novels were passed from hand to hand until they fell apart, read so many times that men memorized entire articles. As night fell, dugouts often came alive with sound: harmonicas, mouth organs, fiddles, or battered guitars playing popular tunes while voices joined in softly. For a few minutes, laughter and music replaced artillery and orders.

35. The Creatures That Thrived in the War

The trenches weren't just filled with soldiers. They were alive with rats, and not the small city kind people imagined back home, but fat, bold, well-fed creatures that grew shockingly large on a constant diet of spilled rations and unburied bodies. Corpses often lay half-buried in the mud for days or weeks between the lines, and rats fed freely, growing sleek and heavy. Many soldiers swore some were "the size of cats," with thick bodies, long tails, and shining eyes that reflected lantern light at night. Men woke to the feeling of something crawling across their chest or face, only to find a rat scrambling away. Others reported the animals gnawing boots, uniforms, bread, and even the fingers of sleeping or dead soldiers.

Their numbers exploded because trench conditions were perfect for breeding. A single female rat can produce 6–10 litters a year, each with 6–12 pups, meaning one pair can theoretically multiply into hundreds within months. With thousands of tons of food waste, human refuse, and bodies scattered along a front that stretched for miles, populations soared into the millions. Some historians estimate that the Western Front may have hosted tens of millions of rats at peak periods. In crowded sectors, soldiers joked that there were more rats than men. Dugouts sometimes seemed to move with them at night, scratching inside walls and burrowing beneath floors.

Attempts to control them rarely worked. Men shot them for sport, clubbed them with shovels, set traps, or kept cats and terriers specifically to hunt them. Entire "rat hunts" were organized during quiet hours, yet by the next night they were back just as thick as before. Beyond the disgust, rats spread disease, contaminated food, and destroyed supplies, chewing through sacks and even electrical or telephone wires.

36. The Creatures That Comforted Soldiers

Animals quietly became part of trench life, and many units adopted unofficial "pets" that offered comfort in a place otherwise stripped of normal affection. Stray dogs wandered into the lines and were quickly fed scraps, given names, and treated like members of the platoon, sleeping beside sentries or following marching columns from trench to trench. Cats were especially valued for hunting the rats that swarmed dugouts and chewed through food and uniforms at night, and soldiers joked that a good trench cat was worth more than an extra ration. Pigeons were treated with near reverence, carefully protected because they often carried the only reliable messages during heavy fighting. One American pigeon, Cher Ami, became famous after being shot through the chest and losing a leg yet still delivering a message that saved nearly two hundred trapped soldiers, earning a medal for bravery. In quieter sectors, men even kept goats, chickens, or ducks taken from nearby farms for eggs, milk, or simply companionship. Units painted mascots on trench signs and dugout doors (bulldogs, goats, horses, or cartoon rats) and posed proudly for photographs beside their animals. In a landscape dominated by mud, wire, and artillery, caring for something small and alive gave soldiers a rare reminder of home, responsibility, and tenderness.

37. When War Messages Flew on Wings

Messenger pigeons became so important to the war that armies treated them almost like another branch of the signal corps. By some estimates, more than 500,000 pigeons were used across the Western Front, housed in mobile lofts, trucks, and wooden coops behind the lines. When telephone wires were cut by shellfire and runners were shot crossing open ground, these birds often became the fastest and most reliable way to send coordinates, artillery requests, or pleas for rescue. Small message slips were tucked into metal capsules attached to their legs, and the pigeons, trained to return instinctively to their home lofts, flew low and fast over trenches and smoke. Their value quickly made them targets. German units reportedly trained hawks and falcons to intercept carrier pigeons midair, turning parts of the sky into strange, silent dogfights between birds. Soldiers sometimes watched helplessly as a message disappeared in a sudden burst of feathers. In a war dominated by machines and artillery, it was often these fragile animals, beating their wings over no man's land, that carried the information that kept entire units alive.

38. A Simple Trick to Detect Deadly Gas

Animals were sometimes used in even stranger ways when it came to surviving chemical warfare. After poison gas attacks, soldiers had to clean and refill their gas masks carefully, but contaminated water could leave invisible traces of chlorine or other toxins that were still deadly to breathe. In some sectors, units kept small goldfish in jars or tins as crude living detectors. Before using a batch of water to wash masks or equipment, they would drop a fish inside and wait. If the fish quickly died or floated to the surface, the water was considered unsafe. If it survived, the water was likely clean enough to use. It was a simple, improvised test that required no instruments or chemicals, just a fragile creature reacting faster than any human could.

39. How War Dogs Delivered Critical Orders

Some trench dogs were more than mascots, they were trained messengers that carried information across the battlefield faster and more safely than most human runners. Signal units selected intelligent, athletic breeds like collies, sheepdogs, or Airedales and trained them to shuttle between two specific handlers rather than roam freely. Each dog bonded with both men, learning their scents and locations, then practiced running back and forth repeatedly for food rewards until the route became instinct. When needed, a small metal tube or leather pouch containing written messages was clipped to the dog's collar, and the animal was released. Staying low to the ground and moving quickly through shell holes, mud, and broken wire, the dogs were far less visible targets than soldiers standing upright. Unlike pigeons, they could run both directions, carrying replies back just as easily. In battles where telephone wires were constantly cut and human runners were often shot, these quiet four-legged couriers sometimes proved the most reliable link between isolated units.

40. War Dogs Searching for Injured Soldiers

Some trench dogs served an even more lifesaving role as so-called "casualty dogs," trained not just to carry messages but to help the wounded. Instead of message tubes, these dogs wore small saddlebags or pouches filled with bandages, water, and basic medical supplies. During or after attacks, they were sent out across shell holes and broken wire to search for injured soldiers lying between the lines. Moving low to the ground and harder to spot than human stretcher-bearers, the dogs could reach places too dangerous for medics under fire. A wounded man might suddenly hear panting in the mud beside him and find a dog carrying the first bandage or drink he'd had in hours. Some animals were trained to stay with the injured and bark or return to guide stretcher teams back to their location.

41. Capturing Small Moments in the Trenches

Cameras were surprisingly rare in the trenches, and most of the photographs people see today were taken not by ordinary soldiers but by official military photographers or newspaper correspondents. Armies tightly controlled photography, fearing that images of defenses, casualties, or troop locations could help the enemy or damage morale at home. Large, fragile cameras were expensive and awkward to carry, and many units banned them near the front lines altogether. A few officers or wealthier soldiers owned small pocket cameras, sometimes smuggling them into the trenches despite regulations, but getting caught could mean confiscation. As a result, most personal photos were taken during quieter moments behind the lines: groups of friends posing beside dugouts, men grinning with trench pets, homemade signs nailed to walls, or muddy "souvenirs" held up like trophies. Combat itself was rarely captured. Instead, the surviving pictures show laughter, boredom, and ordinary faces, small frozen moments of normal life in the middle of an extraordinary war.

42. The Constant Itch of Trench Life

Hygiene in the trenches was a constant losing battle, and lice quickly became one of the most universal enemies soldiers faced. The insects thrived in damp uniforms, crowded dugouts, and weeks without proper washing, hiding in seams and multiplying faster than men could remove them. Soldiers called them "chats," and the daily ritual of picking them out of clothing became known simply as "chatting." Men sat in small groups during quiet moments, turning their shirts inside out and crushing lice between their thumbnails with soft popping sounds, sometimes joking about it like a routine chore. Baths were rare near the front, often limited to a quick splash from a helmet or a shared bucket of cold water, and uniforms might not be properly cleaned for weeks. When units rotated to rest areas, clothes were sometimes passed through improvised steam disinfectors or "delousing stations," but reinfestation happened almost immediately back in the trenches. The itching could be relentless, keeping men awake at night and leaving red welts across their bodies. Many veterans later joked that the lice were the only army that truly occupied the trenches full time.

43. Broken Sleep in a World of Shellfire

Sleep in the trenches was shallow, fragmented, and rarely lasted more than a few hours at a time. Most units rotated through a rough cycle to prevent complete exhaustion: about four to eight days in the front line, several days in support trenches just behind it, and then a week or more in reserve or rest areas before returning forward again. Even so, "rest" was relative. In the front line, men usually slept fully dressed in cramped dugouts or against trench walls, boots on, rifles within arm's reach, ready to move instantly. Dawn and dusk "stand-to" alerts meant everyone was awake before sunrise and again at sunset, while sentry duty required soldiers to take turns watching the parapet in one or two hour shifts through the night. Shellfire, rats, lice, and cold water dripping from trench roofs regularly interrupted whatever sleep they managed. A good night might mean four broken hours; a bad one meant none at all. Only when rotated far to the rear could men finally stretch out on real beds or barn floors and sleep deeply, sometimes for half a day straight, as their bodies tried to repay weeks of accumulated exhaustion.

44. Inside the Giant Trench System

The scale of the trench system itself was almost impossible to imagine. By the later years of the war, the Western Front contained an estimated 25,000 miles of trenches, enough to stretch completely around the Earth. These weren't just single ditches but tangled networks of front lines, support trenches, reserve lines, and communication trenches branching like roots across fields and forests. Some sectors resembled underground towns, with dugouts, kitchens, aid posts, and supply stores carved into the walls. Maps often looked less like battle plans and more like subway diagrams. Maintaining this vast maze required constant labor, with soldiers digging, reinforcing, draining, and rebuilding day and night as rain, shellfire, and collapse destroyed sections faster than they could be repaired.

45. Life Behind the Front Line

Within that vast network, life was organized in layers rather than a single trench. Behind the front line, the battlefield unfolded in layers rather than a single trench. The support trench usually sat about 100–300 yards (90–275 meters) behind the firing line and looked similar but slightly less exposed. It was connected by narrow communication trenches and held reserve troops, ammunition stores, and medical aid posts. Shelling still reached it regularly, but it was somewhat safer and deeper, with more dugouts where men could sleep briefly or wait for orders. Farther back lay the reserve area, often 1–3 miles (1.5–5 kilometers) from the front. Here, trenches gave way to ruined villages, barns, tents, or makeshift camps where soldiers could wash, drill, receive mail, or rest more fully. Although called "rest," these zones were still within artillery range during major offensives and were crowded, noisy, and tense. Only beyond this, sometimes 5–10 miles (8–16 kilometers) behind the lines, did true rear areas exist, where men might sleep indoors, bathe properly, and feel briefly removed from the war. For most soldiers, life moved constantly back and forth through these layers, never far from danger, but always hoping the next step backward would last just a little longer.

46. Laughing at War in Trench Papers

When units rotated into quieter support or reserve areas, some soldiers even created their own homemade "trench newspapers," handwritten or typed sheets passed around like underground magazines to entertain bored troops. Using scavenged paper, pencils, or battered typewriters, men filled the pages with jokes, cartoons, fake advertisements, sports scores, and sarcastic articles about daily life. Headlines might mock rations, complain about the weather, or tease officers with tongue-in-cheek reports like "Mud Expected to Continue Indefinitely" or "General Promises Dry Trenches by 1925." Regular features included poetry, gossip, letters from readers, and humorous advice columns. Some units gave their papers grand names like *The Wipers Times*, *The Mud Lark*, or *The Listening Post*, parodying real newspapers back home. Copies were read aloud in dugouts or shared until they fell apart, giving soldiers something to laugh about in a place where laughter was rare. In the middle of a mechanized war, these fragile, hand-made papers became small acts of creativity and rebellion, proof that humor could survive even in the trenches.

47. Cleanliness as Survival in the Trenches

Staying clean in the trenches required constant improvisation, because proper washing facilities were almost nonexistent near the front. Most soldiers went days or even weeks without a real bath, relying instead on helmets or mess tins filled with cold water scooped from barrels or rain puddles to splash their faces and hands. Shaving, however, was often treated as a necessity rather than a luxury. After poison gas attacks became common, armies learned that gas masks only worked if the rubber seal pressed directly against bare skin, and even a short beard or heavy stubble could let deadly fumes leak inside. For that reason, many men were expected to remain clean-shaven, scraping their faces daily with dull razors, sometimes dry or with only a thin smear of soap, using small mirrors hung from trench walls or the reflection in a bayonet blade. Officers occasionally inspected for stubble, knowing that a missed shave could cost lives. Between washes, soldiers knocked mud from uniforms by beating them against sandbags, dried socks over candles or braziers, and picked out lice from seams by hand. When units finally rotated to the rear, makeshift bathhouses sometimes appeared (rows of tubs, hoses, or steam boilers where dozens of men washed quickly while their clothes were sent through hot "delousing" ovens to kill insects). The process was rushed and rarely comfortable, but even five minutes of warm water, a clean shirt, and a fresh shave could feel transformative. In a world of mud, sweat, and smoke, small acts of cleanliness weren't vanity, they were morale, health, and sometimes survival.

48. Souvenirs Forged From Shell Casings

Even in the middle of destruction, soldiers found ways to create small pieces of art, turning the debris of war into personal souvenirs. Empty shell casings, bullet cartridges, and scrap metal were hammered, carved, or polished into keepsakes during quiet hours. Men engraved names, dates, hometowns, or unit badges into brass artillery shells, shaping them into vases, cups, or decorative ornaments to send home. Others carved pipes, walking sticks, or chess pieces from broken wood crates, or etched designs into spent bullets and bayonets. Some stitched patches from old uniforms into makeshift flags or painted trench signs to mark their dugouts with nicknames and mascots. These handmade objects became tokens of survival, proof that they had endured something unimaginable. Many were mailed back to families or carried home in kit bags after the war, sitting later on mantelpieces or shelves as silent reminders that even surrounded by mud and machinery, soldiers still felt the urge to build something with their hands rather than destroy.

49. Improvising to Survive in the Trenches

Life in the trenches constantly forced soldiers to become inventors, and many small, improvised tools made the difference between misery and survival. Because raising your head above the parapet could mean a sniper's bullet, men built simple periscopes from scraps of wood, wire, and shaving mirrors, allowing them to look over the top safely without exposing themselves. Flooded trenches turned the ground into knee-deep mud, so units laid wooden "duckboards" (narrow slatted walkways) along the bottom to keep boots out of standing water and reduce cases of trench foot. Empty ration tins became stoves, cut and punched with holes to hold small fires or solid fuel tablets for heating tea or soup. Broken bayonets doubled as knives or tools, shell crates were turned into shelves and furniture, and sandbags stuffed with straw became crude mattresses. Communication trenches were reinforced with scavenged doors and beams from ruined houses, while old wire, metal scraps, and anything not nailed down found a second life as hooks, braces, or repairs. In a landscape where official supplies rarely solved everyday problems, soldiers learned to fix, build, and improvise constantly, turning the wreckage of war into the small inventions that kept them alive.

FOUR

Weapons, Machines & Battlefield Weirdness

World War I was a time of incredible and often terrifying invention. As the stalemate in the trenches dragged on, both sides raced to create new technologies that could break the deadlock. This led to the birth of massive machines, strange new weapons, and experimental tools that had never been seen on a battlefield before. This chapter looks at the reality of these inventions, from the first clumsy tanks and early airplanes to the unusual and often surprising ways that soldiers used technology to try and gain an advantage. It was a period where the traditional ways of fighting were replaced by a new kind of industrial and scientific warfare.

50. The Longest-Range Gun of World War I

In the spring of 1918, the people of Paris began hearing explosions that made no sense. The sky was clear. No enemy aircraft were visible. No artillery batteries were anywhere near the city. Yet, without warning, shells kept crashing into streets and rooftops, killing civilians at random. At first, many believed spies or hidden saboteurs were responsible. Others thought bombs were being dropped from invisible high-altitude planes. The truth turned out to be stranger and more unsettling.

More than 75 miles (120 kilometers) away, hidden deep inside a forest, German engineers had built an enormous supergun so large it required special railway tracks just to position it. The barrel stretched over 100 feet long, longer than a blue whale, and fired shells so fast and so high that they briefly entered the upper atmosphere before curving back down toward Paris. For a few seconds after firing, there was no sound at all. Only later would a faint rumble arrive, followed by a sudden explosion. The delay made the shells feel as if they were falling from nowhere. Each shot required precise calculations for wind, rotation of the Earth, and air pressure, making it one of the most advanced artillery experiments of the entire war.

The weapon, later nicknamed the "Paris Gun," was powerful but wildly impractical. Its barrel wore out quickly and had to be replaced after only a few dozen shots, accuracy was poor, and the shells caused more psychological fear than military damage. Still, the effect on the population was enormous. A city that believed itself safely behind the front lines suddenly realized nowhere was truly out of reach. Even hundreds of miles away, the war could still find you.

51. The Chaotic Birth of Tank Warfare

When tanks first appeared on the battlefield in 1916, many soldiers expected them to be unstoppable metal monsters that would roll straight through enemy lines. On paper, they looked revolutionary: armored, armed with cannons and machine guns, able to crush barbed wire and cross trenches that trapped ordinary infantry. But the reality was far messier. Early tanks were slow, unreliable machines that broke down almost as often as they fought. Engines overheated within minutes, tracks snapped in mud, gears jammed, and some vehicles simply stalled before even reaching the front. During their first major use at the Battle of the Somme, many never made it out of their starting positions. Others crawled forward at walking speed, sometimes barely 3 or 4 miles per hour (5–6 kilometers per hour), easy targets for artillery.

Inside, conditions were miserable. Crews worked in deafening noise, choking fumes, and extreme heat that could climb above 120°F (50°C). The air filled with smoke, oil vapor, and cordite from their own guns. There was no suspension, so every shell hole slammed the men against the metal walls. Drivers steered half-blind through tiny slits while mechanics constantly hammered at failing engines mid-battle. Some tanks became stuck in mud so deep that crews simply abandoned them and walked back. Others accidentally drove into shell craters or broke through weak ground and tipped sideways like stranded ships.

Yet even when they barely functioned, their psychological effect was enormous. Enemy troops who had never seen anything like them sometimes fled at the sight of these lumbering steel boxes creeping through the fog. Over time the technology improved, but the first tanks were less sleek war machines and more experimental tractors bolted together under pressure. They represented the awkward birth of modern armored warfare, powerful in theory but, at first, just as likely to defeat themselves as the enemy.

52. A Weapon of Fire and Fear

While engineers experimented with giant superguns and unreliable tanks, the Germans also introduced a far more primitive and terrifying weapon for close combat: the flamethrower. First deployed in 1915, it looked less like advanced technology and more like something from a nightmare. Operators carried heavy metal fuel tanks strapped to their backs, weighing 45–65 pounds (20–30 kilograms), connected by hoses to a long nozzle that blasted a jet of burning fuel when ignited. But the weapon's power came with limits. Most early flamethrowers only held enough fuel for about 10 to 20 seconds of continuous fire. That meant each burst had to count. A few seconds of flame, then silence. Then either the trench was cleared, or the operator was dangerously exposed.

In the tight, narrow spaces of trench warfare, those few seconds could be devastating. Fire curled over sandbags, poured into dugouts, and set wooden supports ablaze almost instantly. Smoke swallowed the air. Men had nowhere to run. Even seasoned troops sometimes fled at the mere sight of a flamethrower team advancing. The psychological effect was enormous. The hiss of pressurized fuel followed by a sudden wall of fire often caused panic long before the flames reached anyone.

Yet carrying one was among the most dangerous jobs on the battlefield. The large fuel tank made the operator an obvious target, and a single bullet could rupture the pack and turn the soldier into an explosion of fire. Because of this, flamethrowers were never common weapons. They were issued only to small specialist assault teams, often volunteers or carefully chosen troops known for their nerve. Many saw it as either an elite role or a near-suicidal one. Used sparingly during raids or breakthroughs, they were designed less for sustained fighting and more for shock and terror. Though rare compared to rifles or artillery, the flamethrower earned an outsized reputation, becoming one of the most feared sights of the entire war.

53. The Deadly Evolution of Gas Warfare

Not every invention tested in World War I was a breakthrough. In fact, many were borderline absurd. Desperate to cross no man's land without being cut down by machine guns, some soldiers were issued heavy armored shields mounted on small wheels, meant to be pushed forward as portable cover. On paper they looked like mobile walls of steel. In reality they were slow, clumsy, and rattled loudly over broken ground, snagging on wire and sinking into mud until the men behind them were left struggling and exposed, easy targets for enemy fire. Other units experimented with early "land torpedoes," small tracked machines packed with explosives that crawled toward enemy trenches by remote control or long wires. Many flipped over in shell holes, got tangled, or exploded too soon, sometimes killing the very soldiers who launched them.

Elsewhere, engineers tried all sorts of desperate contraptions that sounded clever in workshops but fell apart the moment they touched the battlefield. Some units experimented with crude trench catapults, wooden or metal frames with springs or counterweights designed to hurl grenades or bundles of explosives farther than a man could throw. In theory they would let soldiers bombard enemy trenches safely from cover. In practice they were slow to reload, wildly inaccurate, and often snapped or jammed after a few shots, sometimes sending explosives tumbling backward into their own lines.

Others built mechanical digging machines, squat metal devices fitted with blades or rotating scoops that were supposed to carve new trenches automatically while shielding the operator. On paper they promised to save hours of backbreaking labor. But the engines clogged with mud, the gears jammed with stones, and the machines frequently stalled or broke down under shellfire. Soldiers quickly discovered it was faster and safer to use an ordinary shovel.

Personal protection experiments were just as awkward. Some troops were issued improvised body armor made from steel plates sewn into vests or strapped to their chests and backs. The armor could sometimes stop shrapnel or a glancing bullet, but it weighed around 60–70 pounds (27–32 kilograms) and trapped heat against the body. After a few minutes of climbing out of trenches or running across open ground, men were gasping for breath and shedding the plates just to move properly. Protection meant nothing if you couldn't run.

Strange wheeled machines, oversized shields, and homemade devices appeared briefly along the front lines like mechanical curiosities, only to vanish just as quickly. Axles snapped, engines overheated, wheels sank axle-deep into mud, and anything heavier than a man quickly became dead weight.

54. The Poison Gas Arms Race

As the war dragged on, poison gas didn't remain a single terrifying experiment but evolved into a grim chemical arms race. After the first chlorine clouds rolled across the trenches in 1915, both sides began racing to develop new substances that were deadlier, harder to detect, and more difficult to defend against. Phosgene soon replaced chlorine as the primary killer. It was almost invisible and smelled faintly of hay or freshly cut grass, harmless enough that many soldiers removed their masks too early, only to collapse hours later as their lungs slowly filled with fluid. Later came mustard gas, which attacked not just the lungs but the skin and eyes, seeping into clothing and lingering in mud for days. Men who thought they had escaped an attack sometimes woke covered in painful yellow blisters, temporarily blinded or burned raw from the inside out. Unlike earlier gases, mustard didn't always kill quickly, but it filled hospitals with thousands of long-term casualties, overwhelming medical systems and keeping soldiers out of the fight for weeks or months.

Delivery methods grew just as sophisticated. Early attacks relied on large cylinders opened when the wind blew in the right direction, but this was unreliable and sometimes blew gas back onto the attackers themselves. Soon armies switched to artillery shells filled with chemicals, allowing gas to be fired directly onto enemy positions with precision, day or night, regardless of wind. Mortars, rockets, and special projectors spread clouds suddenly and without warning, mixing gas shells with normal high explosives so soldiers never knew what was coming next. Some bombardments layered different chemicals together, forcing troops to keep masks on for hours until exhaustion set in. By the later years of the war, entire barrages were designed not to kill outright but to contaminate trenches, roads, and supply routes, turning the environment itself hostile. The battlefield no longer felt like just mud and wire. The air, the ground, and even the rain could burn or suffocate. Chemistry had become as much a weapon as bullets or shells, and every breath carried uncertainty.

55. Turning Night into Day on the Battlefield

To counter or conceal movement, armies also created artificial weather. Smoke shells and canisters poured thick white or gray clouds across the battlefield, hiding advancing troops, masking retreats, or blinding enemy machine gunners. Entire attacks unfolded inside rolling walls of smoke, where men could barely see a few yards ahead and often stumbled into shell holes or even their own barbed wire.

At night, communication often depended on signal flares and "Very lights," small pistol-like launchers that fired colored stars high above the trenches. These bursts weren't meant to illuminate the battlefield so much as to send urgent messages when telephones were cut and runners couldn't get through. Every unit memorized a simple code. A red flare might mean "enemy attack" or "send help immediately," green could signal "objective taken" or "lift the barrage," (which meant stop firing on friendly positions) and other combinations marked positions, called for reinforcements, or warned of gas. Officers kept flare pistols tucked into their belts like sidearms, ready to fire a message skyward in seconds.

Because so much depended on these signals, mistakes could be deadly. Smoke, stress, or poor timing sometimes led to the wrong color going up, or two flares being mistaken for three. Artillery batteries miles away might respond instantly, shells landing on the wrong trench simply because a signal was misread. Entire attacks occasionally stalled or advanced based on one brief flash of color. Over time, soldiers grew used to glancing upward automatically whenever a flare hissed into the air, reading the sky the way others read a map. In a war where wires were constantly cut and radios unreliable, these tiny sparks became the army's emergency language, quick, crude, and sometimes the only thing keeping chaos from taking over. Soldiers joked that the front never truly slept, because the sky was always flickering with color.

56. Turning Night into Day on the Battlefield

Night fighting was so dangerous and confusing that armies tried to cheat the darkness itself. One of the simplest but most dramatic inventions was the parachute flare. Fired high into the sky from special pistols or mortars, the flare burst open with a sharp crack and released a burning magnesium light suspended beneath a small silk parachute. Instead of falling quickly, it drifted slowly downward, flooding the battlefield with an eerie white glow that could last nearly a minute. For those seconds, no man's land looked like midday. Every crater, strand of barbed wire, and moving figure became sharply visible. Soldiers caught advancing across open ground suddenly found themselves frozen in bright light, their shadows stretching long behind them like targets painted on the earth. Night raids that depended on stealth could collapse instantly when a single flare hissed overhead. Men learned to dive flat and stay perfectly still, praying the light would drift past without revealing them. What had begun as darkness for protection became a stage spotlight, and the sky itself turned into a weapon.

57. Smoke, Flares, and the Battlefield Sky

Long before radar existed, armies tried to hunt enemies in the sky and darkness with pure light. Massive electric searchlights, some more than 3 feet (1 meter) wide across the lens, were mounted on trucks or concrete platforms behind the lines and powered by noisy generators. At night, crews swung their beams slowly across the sky, sweeping back and forth like enormous white fingers. When the light caught something, a Zeppelin, a bomber, or even drifting smoke, the beam locked onto it and tracked it relentlessly. Other lights joined in, crossing their rays until the target was trapped inside a glowing cage of light. From the ground, the sky looked like a theater stage, crisscrossed with bright columns. For the aircraft crews above, it was terrifying. One moment they were hidden in darkness, the next they were fully exposed, every wing and rivet visible, anti-aircraft guns immediately opening fire. Some pilots said being caught in a searchlight felt like being pinned by a spotlight with the whole world shooting at you. The same lights were sometimes turned toward no man's land to illuminate night patrols or expected attacks, transforming muddy fields into harsh, ghostly landscapes where nothing could hide.

58. Listening for the Enemy Before Radar

Before radar could see the enemy, armies tried to hear them first. Along quiet stretches of the front, strange metal horns, wooden funnels, and giant concrete "ears" appeared, looking more like oversized musical instruments than weapons. These listening devices were built to capture the faintest distant sounds: the rumble of trucks, the clank of tanks, the buzz of aircraft engines, or the deep thud of enemy artillery firing miles away. Operators wearing headphones sat perfectly still, turning the horns slowly like telescopes for the ears, trying to pinpoint direction by sound alone. Some horns were small enough to carry; others were enormous, fixed structures several feet wide. On the British coast, huge curved concrete walls called acoustic mirrors were even constructed to reflect the noise of approaching

Zeppelins and bombers toward microphones, giving defenders a few extra minutes of warning.

At the front, a related system called "sound ranging" became surprisingly scientific. Microphones were spread out along the line and connected by cables. When an enemy gun fired, the boom reached each microphone at slightly different times. By measuring those tiny differences, sometimes fractions of a second, technicians could triangulate the exact position of the gun and relay coordinates to their own artillery for counterfire. Entire batteries were located and destroyed this way without ever being seen. It felt almost magical to soldiers: guns hidden behind hills suddenly shelled with uncanny accuracy.

59. An Unusual Vehicle of the War

Not every soldier moved by truck or horse. In many sectors, especially early in the war, armies experimented with bicycle infantry, troops who could travel faster than marching men but far more quietly and cheaply than motor vehicles. Soldiers rode sturdy military bicycles reinforced with thicker frames, tool kits, and racks for rifles and packs, sometimes even fitted with folding designs so they could be carried over obstacles or slung across the back. On paved roads or firm ground, a cyclist could cover two or three times the distance of a marching column while using far less energy, arriving less exhausted and ready to fight. Units used them for scouting, message carrying, rapid reinforcements, and quick flanking movements where surprise mattered more than firepower.

Bicycles were nearly silent compared to engines, making them ideal for night movement or slipping along tree-lined roads without alerting the enemy. Whole platoons could glide forward with only the faint crunch of tires on gravel. But the advantages vanished the moment the terrain turned to mud. Shell holes, barbed wire, churned fields, and shattered forests quickly made riding impossible, forcing men to push or carry the heavy machines instead. Many soldiers joked that their "iron horses" were useful only until the first rainstorm. As the war became more static and the front lines more cratered, bicycles grew less practical, yet they never disappeared entirely. In quieter sectors and rear areas, columns of riflemen pedaling past ruined villages remained a strange sight, half modern and half improvised, proof that even in an industrial war, something as simple as a bicycle could still be a useful piece of military technology.

60. The Daredevils Who Carried the War's Messages

Before radios became reliable, getting a message from one headquarters to another often depended on a single man and a fast engine. Motorcycle dispatch riders became the nervous system of the army, carrying orders, maps, and reports between units when telephone wires were cut by shellfire and runners on foot were too slow or too exposed. Riding lightweight, stripped-down bikes built for rough ground, they sped along muddy roads, through shattered villages, and across open fields under fire, sometimes with leather satchels strapped to their chests or handlebars containing documents that entire battles depended on. A rider might deliver a new attack time, an artillery correction, or a warning that enemy troops were breaking through. If he failed to arrive, hundreds or thousands of men might move at the wrong moment.

The job was notoriously dangerous. Roads near the front were prime targets for artillery, snipers, and aircraft, and dispatch riders often rode alone with no protection. Headlights were dimmed or covered at night to avoid detection, forcing them to navigate by moonlight or memory while dodging shell holes and wrecked wagons. Many bikes skidded in mud or broke down under constant strain, and riders sometimes had to abandon the machine and run the last stretch on foot. Casualty rates were high enough that the role earned a grim reputation, yet volunteers kept stepping forward, drawn by the speed and independence of the work. Soldiers joked that dispatch riders lived fast and died young, but they also knew these lone motorcyclists were often the difference between chaos and coordination.

61. Motorcycle Machine-Gun Teams

As armies searched for ways to add speed and firepower to a battlefield that was mostly mud and trenches, some experimented with an odd hybrid between cavalry and early mechanized warfare: motorcycles fitted with sidecars carrying machine guns. These three-wheeled machines looked almost improvised, a roaring bike with a metal tub bolted to the side, but inside the sidecar sat a gunner crouched behind a mounted weapon, often a Lewis gun or Maxim, ready to fire while the driver steered. The idea was simple: move fast, hit hard, and relocate before the enemy could respond. On firm roads or open countryside, these units could race ahead of infantry columns, escort convoys, chase retreating troops, or quickly reinforce weak points.

In theory, they combined the mobility of a motorcycle with the firepower of a machine-gun team. In practice, they were temperamental and risky. The extra weight made steering awkward, especially over ruts or shell holes, and sharp turns could flip the entire machine. Mud clogged wheels, engines overheated, and a single bullet could disable both rider and gunner at once. Once the fighting moved off roads and into cratered no man's land, the sidecars often bogged down completely, becoming little more than expensive targets. Still, in rear areas, deserts, or less damaged sectors, they proved useful for patrols and quick raids, and some armies kept them throughout the war. To soldiers watching them bounce past in clouds of dust, they looked like something from the future, a glimpse of the fast, mechanized warfare that would dominate the next global conflict.

62. The Steel Traps of the Western Front

Long before tanks or flamethrowers changed the battlefield, one of the most effective and feared weapons of World War I was something far simpler: barbed wire. Originally designed for fencing cattle, it became a deadly military tool that shaped almost every trench system on the Western Front. Engineers didn't just string up a few lines. They built vast, tangled belts of wire sometimes 20–50 yards (18–45 meters) deep, layered in overlapping coils, stakes, and spirals known as "concertina" wire. From a distance it looked like messy metal brush. Up close it was a maze of razor-sharp barbs waiting to snag clothing, packs, rifles, or flesh. At night or in fog, soldiers often didn't see it until they were already trapped inside.

These barriers weren't random obstacles but carefully planned killing zones. Machine-gun crews positioned their guns to fire directly over the wire, knowing any attacking soldier slowed down or stuck would become an easy target. Artillery shells frequently failed to cut the thicker strands, leaving gaps too small to crawl through. Men carried heavy wire cutters or special explosives called Bangalore torpedoes, long pipes filled with explosives that were shoved under the wire and detonated to blast a narrow path. Even then, clearing lanes took precious minutes under fire. Many assaults collapsed not because defenders shot everyone immediately, but because attacking waves piled up helplessly in the wire, tangled together while bullets and shells rained down. Survivors described hearing the awful metallic scraping of men struggling to free themselves and the cries of the wounded caught fast.

Maintaining these barriers became constant labor. Patrols repaired damaged sections every night, hammering in new stakes and weaving fresh coils under cover of darkness. By the later years of the war, millions of miles of wire crisscrossed the front, enough to fence entire countries many times over. Some sectors looked less like farmland and more like twisted steel forests. For soldiers, wire became almost as terrifying as artillery itself. You could hide from shells and dodge bullets, but once the wire grabbed you, there was nowhere left to run.

63. The Close-Range Terror of Trench Mortars

Not all artillery fired from miles away. Some of the most feared weapons on the Western Front were squat, ugly tubes that sat only a few hundred yards from the enemy. These were trench mortars, known to the Germans as *minenwerfers* or "mine throwers," short-range weapons designed specifically for the tight, cramped geometry of trench warfare. Instead of long barrels and flat trajectories like traditional guns, they looked like oversized stovepipes or metal drainpipes bolted to a baseplate, angled steeply upward to lob enormous shells high into the air. From a distance they almost looked homemade, like plumbing parts stuck in the mud, but the damage they caused was anything but crude.

Their ammunition was shockingly large for such small weapons. Some shells were the size of a bucket or small barrel, weighing 20–100 pounds (9–45 kilograms) or more, packed with explosives and scrap metal. Because the mortars fired at a steep arc, the bombs dropped almost straight down into trenches, dugouts, and strongpoints that normal artillery often missed. Soldiers quickly learned to fear the sound. Unlike the long whistle of distant artillery, mortar bombs made a dull, slow "plop" or hollow *thunk* as they left the tube, followed by a few seconds of dreadful silence while the shell hung invisibly overhead. Then came a sudden, earth-shaking blast that collapsed trench walls, buried men alive, or blew sandbags and timber into splinters. Veterans said that quiet pause between launch and impact was worse than the explosion itself, giving just enough time to realize something terrible was about to land nearby.

Mortars also had a brutal psychological effect. Because the mortars were positioned so close to the front, crews could often see their targets directly and adjust the angle after each shot, making them far more accurate than distant artillery. After only a few rounds, shells could be dropped almost exactly into a chosen trench bay or dugout entrance, which made the weapon feel personal as well as deadly. Entire sections could disappear in one hit. In response, both sides built their own mortar units, leading to constant back-and-forth bombardments at ranges sometimes shorter than a football field. Crude, heavy, and ugly, trench mortars perfectly matched the nature of the war itself: close, dirty, and devastating.

64. Floating Watchtowers Above the Front

Long before fighter planes ruled the sky, the most important eyes on the battlefield were not aircraft at all but giant hydrogen-filled observation balloons that hovered silently above the trenches like strange gray sea creatures. These were not hot-air balloons with flames, and not true blimps with engines, but tethered "kite balloons," fat sausage-shaped gas bags anchored to the ground by a thick steel cable and raised or lowered by a winch truck. Once inflated with hydrogen, they could climb 3,000–5,000 feet (900–1,500 meters) into the air and remain almost perfectly still for hours, acting like floating watchtowers. From that height, an observer with binoculars could see miles beyond the front lines: gun flashes, moving columns, supply trains, trenches being dug, even men gathering for an attack. What looked hidden from the mud below was completely exposed from above.

Inside the small wicker basket, one or two officers worked like calm air-traffic controllers of destruction. Most communicated through a field telephone line that ran down the tether cable, essentially a wired phone stretching from the sky to the artillery batteries below. Others tapped out Morse code on early wireless radios powered by heavy batteries and generators.

They didn't speak dramatically or shout orders. They simply made tiny corrections: "Left fifty… drop one hundred… fire again." Artillery rarely hit perfectly on the first shot, so each adjustment moved the next shell a little closer, the explosions creeping step by step across the ground. Soldiers called this "walking" the fire, because the blasts seemed to march forward like footsteps in the mud, one impact after another, until they landed directly on a trench, road, or gun position. From above, the observer could literally watch the shells advance toward their target and guide them in with calm, almost casual instructions. Within minutes, guns miles away could zero in with frightening precision. For the first time in history, artillery stopped being blind and became accurate, turning distant cannons into something closer to guided weapons than guesswork.

Because of that deadly precision, balloon crews became some of the most hunted men in the war. Infantry hated seeing an enemy balloon overhead, knowing it meant artillery would soon follow. Snipers couldn't reach them at that height, but artillery targeted the winch trucks and ground crews, and fighter pilots were given special "balloon busting" missions. These attacks were among the most dangerous jobs in the air. Pilots had to dive low through heavy anti-aircraft fire and shoot incendiary bullets into the hydrogen bag. These were special rounds filled with flammable chemicals like phosphorus that ignited on impact, designed not just to pierce fabric but to start fires. Ordinary bullets would only punch small holes and let the gas leak slowly, but incendiaries sparked and burned the instant they struck. When hit, the balloon didn't sag or slowly deflate. It erupted almost instantly into a towering fireball, sometimes hundreds of feet high, the explosion visible for miles across the front.

For that reason, balloon observers were among the first soldiers in the war to routinely carry parachutes. While many fighter pilots early in the war had none at all, balloon crews wore static-line silk chutes packed beside the basket. If flames appeared, they had only seconds to jump. When they did, the parachute snapped open automatically, and men drifted slowly down while their balloon burned above them like a falling sun. The parachutes were surprisingly reliable, often saving lives, but timing mattered. Jump too late, and the silk could catch fire or the blast could flip the basket before escape.

By 1918, hundreds of these balloons dotted the Western Front. In some sectors, they formed entire "balloon lines," rising and lowering throughout the day like mechanical suns. Soldiers learned to glance upward instinctively. If the sky held a gray shape watching them, nowhere felt safe. Even miles behind the trenches, you could still be seen. Many veterans later said the balloons felt worse than airplanes, not because they moved, but because they didn't. They simply hung there, silent and patient, like unblinking eyes tethered to the sky, proving that in modern war, even the clouds were watching.

65. Fooling the Enemy From the Air

As aircraft and observation balloons began watching the front from above, the battlefield became a strange game of deception where looking real could be just as dangerous as being real. Armies quickly learned that anything visible from the sky, guns, roads, supply dumps, even kitchens, could draw artillery within minutes. So soldiers started hiding everything. Nets woven with strips of cloth and burlap were draped over trenches and vehicles to break up their outlines. Mud, branches, and scraps of vegetation were piled onto helmets and guns to make them blend into the ground.

Artillery pieces were painted in blotchy greens and browns or covered with patterned canvas so they looked like patches of earth instead of metal. From the air, a well-camouflaged battery could vanish completely.

But hiding wasn't enough. Soon both sides began building things that were deliberately fake. Dummy cannons made from wood or painted canvas were set up to attract enemy fire away from real guns. Fake horses and supply wagons stood in open fields to suggest troop movements that didn't exist. Engineers dug entire dummy trench systems, complete with sandbags, duckboards, and even smoke from fake cook fires, hoping enemy pilots would photograph and shell empty ground. Some sectors built canvas "tanks" or plywood vehicles that looked convincing from a few thousand feet up but collapsed if touched. In a few cases, fake villages and roads were constructed behind the lines to mislead bombers, complete with painted rooftops and carefully arranged lights at night.

The goal wasn't just concealment but confusion. If the enemy couldn't tell what was real, they wasted shells, time, and aircraft on ghosts. From above, the front sometimes resembled a theatrical stage set, part reality and part illusion.

FIVE

The Hidden War

Beyond the visible battlefields of mud and wire, another kind of conflict was being fought in the shadows. This was a war of secrets, where information was as valuable as ammunition and a single intercepted message could change the fate of an entire army. This chapter looks at the reality of espionage and intelligence, from the daring work of spies and codebreakers to the clever ways that nations tried to hide their plans from the enemy. It was a silent and dangerous struggle that took place in quiet offices, behind enemy lines, and even in the air, proving that some of the most important battles of World War I were the ones that no one ever saw.

66. Spies and Secret Intelligence

Every army built networks of spies, codebreakers, and informants, trying to learn enemy plans while hiding their own. Civilians, shopkeepers, waiters, and railway workers were quietly recruited to watch troop movements or listen for rumors. Letters were intercepted, telegrams copied, and telephone lines tapped. Entire departments existed solely to open mail with steam, read it, reseal it, and send it on without the sender ever knowing. Suspicion spread everywhere. A stranger with a camera, an accent, or a notebook could be arrested on the spot.

Professional spies operated under false names and forged papers, slipping across borders to steal maps or count trains. Some carried invisible ink or hid microfilm inside buttons, shoes, or hollow coins. Others posed as nurses, businessmen, or journalists while secretly passing information at night. Intelligence officers studied aerial photographs, decoded radio signals, and pieced together clues like detectives solving a crime. A single intercepted message could reveal an entire offensive and save thousands of lives. By the end of the war, espionage had grown into a vast, organized system, laying the foundations for the modern intelligence agencies that still operate today.

67. Disguised Observation Posts of the War

Along the Western Front, even the trees could be spies. In some sectors where the ground was too flat or exposed for safe observation, both sides built fake trees that doubled as hidden lookout posts. Engineers studied real, dead tree trunks in no man's land, then carefully removed them at night and replaced them with hollow steel replicas shaped and painted to look identical, complete with fake bark, knots, and broken branches. Inside, just enough space existed for one soldier to climb up and stand with binoculars or a periscope, peering through tiny concealed slits. From a distance, it looked like nothing more than another shattered stump left by shellfire. By day, the observer quietly mapped enemy trenches, counted troop movements, and reported artillery positions. By night, messages were carried back through communication trenches. The job was terrifying. If the enemy noticed movement or suspected the deception, the entire "tree" could be blasted apart by artillery or snipers, trapping the man inside. Yet these disguised posts provided some of the most valuable intelligence on the battlefield, proving that sometimes survival depended less on firepower and more on looking like part of the landscape itself.

68. The Decoy City of Paris

As German bombers began targeting Paris at night, the French came up with a solution that sounded more like stage magic than warfare: they built a fake city to trick enemy pilots. On the outskirts of the real capital, engineers constructed an elaborate decoy "Paris" made from wood, canvas, and painted fabric, complete with imitation streets, rail yards, factories, and even a mock version of the Seine River. At night, hundreds of carefully arranged lights flickered on to mimic neighborhoods, train stations, and moving traffic. Some buildings were only empty frames covered with cloth, just convincing enough from the air to look real. Fake railway lines were built with glowing lamps that simulated trains arriving and departing, while rotating lights copied the patterns of factories working late into the night. From thousands of feet above, through darkness and haze, the illusion was good enough to fool pilots navigating by sight. The hope was simple: bombs dropped on the fake city meant fewer falling on the real one. Although the war ended before the decoy was fully completed and heavily tested, the project remains one of the strangest defensive ideas of the conflict.

69. The Psychological War of Propaganda Leaflets

As the war dragged into its third and fourth years, armies discovered that breaking a soldier's mind could be easier than breaking a trench. Both sides began printing thousands, then millions, of small paper leaflets in the enemy's language and scattering them across the front like artificial snow. Special artillery shells were designed to burst open midair and release clouds of paper instead of shrapnel. Mortars, observation balloons, and even aircraft dropped bundles that fluttered down into trenches and dugouts. The messages were simple and tempting: surrender and you will be fed, kept warm, treated for wounds, and sent safely to a prison camp. Some leaflets showed staged photographs of smiling prisoners of war eating bread, smoking cigarettes, or playing football behind the lines, making captivity look almost comfortable compared to mud and shellfire. Others included "safe conduct passes" that soldiers could carry in their pockets and hold up when approaching enemy lines. Many exaggerated enemy defeats or claimed the war was already lost, quietly planting the idea that further fighting was pointless.

At first, men joked about them or used them as toilet paper, but by 1917–1918, after years of hunger, cold, and failed offensives, the leaflets began to work. Captured soldiers were sometimes found with the passes folded carefully in their tunics. Entire groups surrendered together, stepping out with hands raised rather than die in another assault. In some sectors during the final months, dozens or even hundreds of exhausted German troops gave themselves up in a single day. For many, prison camps meant regular meals, dry beds, and safety from artillery, conditions that could feel better than the front line. Commanders hated the leaflets not because they were laughable, but because they quietly eroded morale and made surrender seem reasonable. It became one of the earliest and most effective forms of large-scale psychological warfare, proving that sometimes a piece of paper could succeed where bullets could not.

70. The Dangerous Power of Battlefield Rumors

In the trenches, information was often scarcer than food. There were no radios, no live reports, and no reliable way for ordinary soldiers to know what was happening even a few miles away, let alone across the front. Newspapers arrived days or weeks late, letters were delayed or censored, and officers rarely shared plans with the ranks. Into that silence poured rumor. News traveled mouth to mouth faster than any official message. A man might hear from a runner that the neighboring regiment had been wiped out, from a letter that the war would end by Christmas, or from a cook that relief was coming tomorrow. By nightfall the story had changed three times. Hopeful rumors spread just as quickly as frightening ones: "We're being pulled out at dawn," "the enemy is retreating," "a breakthrough happened up north," or "fresh Americans are arriving." Others crushed morale overnight: exaggerated casualty lists, claims that an entire brigade had vanished, whispers of unstoppable gas or new super-weapons. Sometimes the gossip turned out to be half-true or even accurate, which made it feel trustworthy; soldiers occasionally heard about real offensives, shortages, or collapses days before official confirmation. Censorship made things worse. Missing details created speculation, and speculation bred wild stories. Men began to believe almost anything: spies everywhere, cursed trenches, lucky charms, even angels protecting the lines. Officers tried to fight the chaos with daily briefings and posted bulletins, but fear and boredom were stronger than facts.

71. The Spy Who Became a Legend

Among the many shadowy figures accused of espionage during the war, none became more famous than Mata Hari, the glamorous dancer who transformed into one of history's most legendary spies. Born Margaretha Zelle in the Netherlands, she reinvented herself in Paris before the war as an exotic performer, adopting the stage name "Mata Hari," meaning "eye of the day" in Malay. Draped in silk and jewels, she captivated wealthy officers, diplomats, and politicians, moving easily through elite circles across Europe. When war broke out, those connections suddenly made her valuable, and dangerous. Traveling between neutral and enemy countries, she accepted money from both French and German intelligence, claiming she was merely gathering gossip, not secrets.

But as the war dragged on and France suffered devastating losses, the government desperately needed someone to blame for military failures. Mata Hari's independence, foreign status, and reputation for seducing officers made her an easy target. Arrested in 1917, she was accused of causing the deaths of thousands of soldiers by passing information to Germany, though historians later found little real evidence that she had ever provided anything important. Her trial was brief and sensational. Newspapers painted her as a deadly femme fatale, a beautiful traitor who used romance as a weapon.

At dawn on October 15, 1917, she faced a firing squad outside Paris. Refusing a blindfold, she reportedly stood straight, dressed elegantly, and blew a final kiss to the soldiers before the shots rang out. Whether master spy or convenient scapegoat, her execution turned her into a symbol of the hidden war.

72. Inside the Hidden World of Wartime Cryptography

While popular imagination pictured spies slipping through shadows with forged passports and secret meetings, much of the real intelligence war happened in quiet rooms filled with desks, maps, and exhausted clerks. Across Europe, armies built entire codebreaking centers where intercepted telegrams and radio signals were sorted, copied, and studied line by line. Operators tapped out enemy messages in Morse code, then teams of linguists, mathematicians, and puzzle-solvers tried to turn the scrambled letters back into meaning. Walls filled with pinned notes, string connections, and half-solved ciphers. The work was slow, repetitive, and maddening, sometimes taking days to decode a single message.

In Britain, a secret unit known as Room 40 intercepted and decrypted thousands of German naval signals, quietly tracking submarine movements and fleet positions. One intercepted telegram, later called the Zimmermann Telegram, revealed Germany's attempt to persuade Mexico to attack the United States, helping push America into the war. No guns were fired, no trenches stormed, yet a few sheets of decoded paper changed the course of history. The people doing this work rarely left their desks and never received medals, but their victories could save more lives than entire divisions.

SIX

Medicine & Survival

The massive scale of World War I forced a revolution in how doctors and nurses cared for the wounded and the sick. On a battlefield where industrial weapons caused injuries never seen before, the struggle to save lives became a race against time and infection. This chapter looks at the reality of medical care during the conflict, from the development of life-saving new techniques to the incredible resilience of those who worked in the shadow of the front lines. It was a time of rapid discovery and immense bravery, where the goal was not just to fight the war, but to survive the devastating toll it took on the human body and mind.

73. The Birth of Modern Battlefield Triage

The chaos of industrial warfare also forced doctors to rethink a brutal question: who should be treated first when hundreds of wounded men arrive at once? Earlier wars often treated soldiers in the order they appeared or by rank, but World War I made that impossible. After major offensives, stretcher-bearers might carry in thousands of casualties within hours, far more than any medical team could handle. Treating everyone equally meant many would die waiting. So military doctors developed a new system called "triage," from the French word trier, meaning "to sort." Instead of first come, first served, the wounded were rapidly divided into categories: those who would survive without help, those too badly injured to save, and those who could live if treated immediately. Resources went to the last group first. It was a cold, mathematical approach to survival, sometimes forcing medics to walk past dying men to reach someone with better odds. Yet the system dramatically increased survival rates, saving thousands who might otherwise have been lost. The method proved so effective that it became standard practice in modern emergency rooms, ambulances, and disaster zones. Every time doctors today prioritize patients after an accident or earthquake, they are using a system forged in the overcrowded field hospitals of World War I.

74. Speed Becomes a Weapon Against Death

Speed often meant the difference between life and death, yet at the start of the war most wounded soldiers were still hauled away in horse-drawn carts little different from those used a century earlier. After battles, stretcher-bearers struggled through mud and shell holes carrying men for miles to reach aid posts, then loaded them onto slow wagons that jolted painfully over rough roads. The journey could take hours. Many soldiers who survived the initial wound simply bled to death before ever reaching a surgeon. As the scale of casualties exploded, armies began replacing horses with motorized ambulances, small petrol-powered vehicles that could weave through damaged roads and reach hospitals far faster than animal teams. For the first time, wounded men could be transported lying flat instead of stacked upright, reducing shock and further injury. Drivers often raced through artillery fire at night with headlights dimmed, knowing every minute counted. Combined with triage and better surgery, these faster evacuations dramatically increased survival rates.

75. A Medical Breakthrough That Saved Thousands

Before World War I, blood transfusions were chaotic and dangerously improvised. If a wounded soldier needed blood, a donor often had to lie beside him while doctors transferred blood directly from one arm to another through rubber tubes. There was no way to store it, no organized supply, and no guarantee the donor's blood type would match. Thousands of men who might have survived simply bled to death because fresh blood wasn't available in time. In 1917, a U.S. Army doctor named Captain Oswald Robertson changed that by creating what is considered the world's first true blood bank. Working near the front lines in France, he collected blood from donors, mixed it with sodium citrate to prevent clotting, and stored it in bottles packed in ice so it could last for days instead of minutes. For the first time, blood could be stockpiled, labeled by type, transported by truck, and given exactly when needed. Robertson's small refrigerated crates followed the fighting like mobile lifelines, supplying surgeons during major battles and saving countless wounded soldiers who would previously have died on the operating table.

76. The Fight Against Deadly Infection

For much of the early war, surviving a bullet or shell wound did not mean surviving the hospital. Infection killed almost as many soldiers as the weapons themselves. Trench mud was thick with manure, bacteria, and rotting debris, and when shrapnel tore through flesh it carried that contamination deep into the body. Even small wounds could turn deadly within days. Limbs swelled, skin blackened, and a sweet, foul smell signaled the arrival of gangrene or blood poisoning. Surgeons often had no choice but to amputate quickly or watch the infection spread. Entire wards filled with men dying not from their injuries, but from what grew inside them afterward. The scale of the problem forced doctors to rethink battlefield hygiene completely. Medical teams began aggressively cleaning and cutting away contaminated tissue, flushing wounds with antiseptic solutions like carbolic acid or diluted bleach, and sterilizing instruments between operations. New methods such as the Carrel-Dakin system continuously dripped disinfectant into deep wounds to kill bacteria before they multiplied. Field hospitals improved handwashing, boiling of bandages, and separation of infected patients. These practices sound basic today, but at the time they were revolutionary. Death rates from infected wounds dropped dramatically, and survival rates soared.

77. When Doctors Could Finally See Inside Wounds

Finding bullets and shrapnel inside the human body used to be a grim guessing game. Surgeons often had to probe blindly with their fingers or knives, searching for metal fragments they couldn't see, sometimes causing more damage than the wound itself. World War I changed that with the introduction of mobile X-ray units, many of them organized by the famous scientist Marie Curie. Realizing that wounded soldiers were dying simply because doctors couldn't locate internal injuries quickly enough, Curie helped design small, portable radiology labs built inside cars and trucks. These vehicles carried X-ray machines, generators, and photographic equipment, allowing doctors to drive directly to field hospitals near the front. Nicknamed "Little Curies," the units glowed faintly in darkened tents as technicians developed images showing bones, bullets, and shrapnel clearly for the first time. Surgeons could suddenly see exactly where to cut instead of guessing, dramatically reducing surgery time and saving countless lives. Curie personally trained dozens of women as radiology operators and even drove some of the vehicles herself. By the end of the war, hundreds of thousands of soldiers had been examined using these mobile X-rays, turning a laboratory discovery into a battlefield lifesaver and laying the groundwork for modern medical imaging used in hospitals today.

78. The Birth of Modern Plastic Surgery

Modern plastic surgery was born not in beauty clinics, but in the shattered trenches of World War I. The nature of trench fighting meant soldiers often exposed only their heads above the parapet, and when artillery shells or sniper bullets struck, they frequently destroyed faces rather than bodies. Thousands of men survived wounds that would have killed them in earlier wars, but they returned with missing jaws, shattered cheekbones, torn noses, or entire sections of their faces blown away. Doctors suddenly faced a problem medicine had never seen on this scale: how to rebuild a human face. At hospitals in Britain and France, surgeons like Harold Gillies began experimenting with revolutionary techniques, grafting skin from a patient's chest or forehead, shaping new noses from cartilage, and inventing the "tube pedicle," a method of moving living skin across the body without cutting off its blood supply. Some soldiers underwent dozens of operations over months or years. Artists even sculpted painted metal or leather masks to cover disfigurements while reconstruction continued. The results were crude by modern standards but miraculous for the time, allowing men to eat, speak, and walk in public again without hiding their faces.

79. Pain and Anesthesia in Field Hospitals

Saving a life did not mean sparing a soldier pain. Field hospitals during World War I were places of relentless suffering, where men arrived with shattered limbs, torn flesh, and faces burned or broken beyond recognition. Surgery was often performed quickly and repeatedly, sometimes with only basic anesthesia, and recovery could be agony. To cope, doctors relied heavily on morphine, chloroform, and ether, powerful drugs that dulled pain but carried their own risks. Small glass morphine syrettes were injected before operations or given to wounded men lying on stretchers, the drug bringing a heavy, floating calm that many described as the only relief they felt for days. For surgeons, morphine felt like a miracle when it was available. Small glass syrettes were injected before operations or given to men lying on stretchers, bringing a heavy, floating calm that dulled the worst of the pain. But supplies were never guaranteed. During major battles, when hundreds or thousands arrived at once, drugs ran short and doses were rationed carefully. Some men went into surgery sedated; others endured procedures with only chloroform, ether, or nothing stronger than a leather strap to bite down on. In overcrowded wards lit by lanterns and filled with groans, nurses sometimes had to hold patients still while surgeons worked as quickly as they could.

80. Learning to Walk Again After the War

Saving a soldier's life was only the first step. For tens of thousands of survivors, the war had taken an arm or a leg, and returning home meant learning how to live inside a permanently altered body. Before World War I, most prosthetic limbs were crude wooden pegs or simple hooks, heavy, uncomfortable, and more symbolic than useful. But the sheer number of amputees forced rapid innovation. Hospitals and workshops began designing lighter artificial legs with hinged knees and ankles, shaped sockets that fit the body more naturally, and straps that allowed men to walk with something close to a normal gait. Artificial arms evolved from stiff wooden blocks into mechanical hands with moving fingers, cables, and springs that could grip tools, hold cups, or even write. Entire rehabilitation centers were created where veterans practiced walking, climbing stairs, or relearning trades like carpentry and typing. For the first time, prosthetics weren't just replacements, they were engineered for function.

81. Fighting War With Toothache

Not every medical problem in the trenches came from bullets or shells. Sometimes the most disabling enemy was a simple toothache. Soldiers lived on hard biscuits, tough salted meat, sugary tea, and constant tobacco, rarely brushing and almost never seeing a dentist. Cavities, abscesses, and broken teeth became common, and without treatment the pain could be unbearable. A man might be unable to sleep, eat, or even hold a rifle steady, effectively removing him from duty as surely as a wound. Early in the war, thousands of soldiers were evacuated from the front for dental problems alone, clogging hospitals with cases that had nothing to do with combat. Armies soon realized they were losing more manpower to teeth than to some minor battles. In response, they created mobile field dentistry units, small tents or trucks where dentists worked near the front lines extracting teeth, filling cavities, and fitting crude dentures. The solution was often blunt and fast: if a tooth hurt, it came out. Rows of men sometimes lined up outside aid posts waiting their turn, gripping chairs while dentists pulled teeth in minutes before sending them straight back to duty. It was painful and primitive, but effective. By the end of the war, organized military dentistry had become standard, laying the foundation for modern army dental corps.

82. Nurses on the Front Lines of Medicine

While new technologies like blood banks, X-rays, and ambulances transformed battlefield medicine, much of the real work of saving lives fell to exhausted nurses working in fragile hospitals just behind the front. These were rarely solid buildings. Most were canvas tents, wooden huts, or barns hastily converted into wards, their floors muddy, their roofs leaking, and their walls rattling whenever artillery boomed nearby. Inside, rows of stretchers lay shoulder to shoulder, often so tightly packed that staff had to turn sideways just to squeeze between them. Lanterns or weak electric bulbs cast a yellow glow over makeshift operating tables built from wooden doors balanced on crates. The air smelled of blood, antiseptic, wet wool, and smoke. Boots never fully dried, and everything felt permanently damp.

When major offensives began, the wounded arrived in waves that didn't stop for days. Ambulances and stretcher-bearers unloaded men faster than beds could be cleared. Nurses cleaned mud and lice from uniforms, cut away clothing stiff with blood, washed wounds, held down screaming patients during surgery, and carried buckets of water back and forth until their arms shook. Shifts stretched to 18 or even 20 hours at a time, with only minutes to sit or eat. Many learned to nap standing against a wall between cases. Some wrote final letters home for dying soldiers who could no longer hold a pen, or simply sat beside them so they wouldn't be alone. For countless men, the first gentle voice they heard after being hit belonged not to a doctor, but to a nurse offering water or calling them "love."

These hospitals were not safe havens. They were often still within artillery range, and shells sometimes landed close enough to shatter windows or collapse tents. Nurses were killed or wounded while tending patients, yet many refused to move farther back, knowing every extra mile of transport meant more soldiers dying before reaching care. In a war dominated by machinery, steel, and mass destruction, their work was intensely personal: hands bandaging, hands lifting, hands comforting. Long after the war, veterans remembered the faces of the nurses who treated them more clearly than the generals who commanded them.

SEVEN

Prisoners of War

For many soldiers, the war did not end on the battlefield, but in the hands of the enemy. Being captured was a sudden and life-changing event that turned a fighter into a prisoner, often for years at a time. This chapter looks at the reality of life behind the wire, from the initial shock of being taken to the daily struggle of living in crowded camps. It was a unique and difficult experience where survival depended on patience, resilience, and the hope of one day returning home to a world that was changing without them.

83. Surrender and Survival in the Trenches

Most prisoners of war were not captured in dramatic last-stand battles but during the quieter, more chaotic moments when units broke, got lost, or were simply surrounded. In trench warfare, entire sections of line could collapse in minutes. A failed attack might leave survivors stranded in shell holes with no officers and no ammunition. When artillery cut telephone wires and smoke covered the battlefield, men often had no idea where friendly lines even were. Some wandered straight into enemy trenches by mistake. Others were cut off when flanking units retreated. During large offensives, thousands surrendered at once when resistance became pointless. Machine-gun crews out of bullets, stretcher-bearers caught in the open, and exhausted soldiers trapped behind new enemy positions often raised their hands rather than die needlessly.

The scale was enormous. By the end of the war, roughly 8 to 9 million soldiers worldwide had become prisoners. Germany alone held about 2.5 to 3 million captives, many of them Russians. Russia captured roughly 2 to 2.5 million Austro-Hungarian and German troops. Austria-Hungary held around 1 to 1.5 million, mostly Russians and Italians. Britain and France together held hundreds of thousands more, including Ottoman and German soldiers. Some single battles produced staggering numbers. At Tannenberg in 1914, tens of thousands of Russians were captured in days. During the final Allied offensives of 1918, entire German units surrendered by the thousands as morale collapsed. For many men, becoming a prisoner wasn't a heroic last moment but a simple calculation: wounded, hungry, and surrounded, captivity meant survival.

84. Life Outside the Prison Camps

Many prisoners were assigned to labor detachments rather than kept inside main camps. Captives were sent out in small groups to farms, mines, factories, and rail yards, where they worked under guard but often interacted directly with civilians. In agricultural regions especially, prisoners sometimes lived in barns or village quarters instead of fenced compounds. For farmers facing labor shortages, these men became essential workers, blurring the line between enemy soldier and temporary employee.

85. Hunger and Hope in Prison Camps

Food quickly became the central obsession of prisoner-of-war camp life, because rations were designed only to keep men barely alive, not healthy. A typical daily issue in many German camps might be thin turnip or cabbage soup, a chunk of coarse black bread weighing about half a pound (225 grams), and sometimes a small portion of potatoes or barley. Meat was rare, often just scraps of fat or gristle floating in broth. Coffee was usually a bitter substitute made from roasted acorns or chicory. Many prisoners consumed fewer than 1,000–1,400 calories a day, far below what a working adult needed, and weight loss was constant. Men grew hollow-cheeked and weak, and conversations revolved endlessly around food: what they missed, what they would eat first at home, or imaginary recipes made from memory.

Because official rations were so poor, parcels from home became lifesavers rather than luxuries. Families, charities, and organizations like the Red Cross shipped millions of packages containing real bread, tinned beef, jam, chocolate, condensed milk, tea, sugar, butter, sausages, or biscuits. A single

Red Cross parcel could provide several days' worth of proper calories. Camps often allowed one parcel per man per week if transport lines were functioning. Prisoners guarded these boxes fiercely, trading items like currency or pooling ingredients to cook shared meals on small improvised stoves. Entire barracks might celebrate the arrival of one intact parcel, turning a tin of jam or slab of chocolate into an event that lifted morale more than any speech.

Letters followed a similar path. Mail was censored but usually permitted under the Geneva Convention. Prisoners wrote home on thin, preprinted cards with limited space and strict rules about what they could say. Messages traveled through camp post offices, then by rail and ship through neutral countries before reaching families. Delivery could take weeks or months, but even a short note in familiar handwriting was priceless. Men reread letters until the paper wore thin, memorizing every line. In a world of barbed wire and hunger, food parcels fed the body, but letters fed something just as important; the stubborn hope that life still existed beyond the fence.

86. Escape Attempts from Prison Camps

Escape attempts ranged from impulsive sprints toward nearby woods to carefully planned operations that took months to prepare. Prisoners dug tunnels beneath fences, forged documents, disguised themselves as laborers, or slipped away during work details. Most attempts failed, often ending with recapture within days. Yet the idea of escape mattered psychologically, giving prisoners a sense of agency in a situation otherwise defined by powerlessness.

87. Trade and Barter Behind Barbed Wire

Camps developed their own internal economies. Cigarettes, bread, soap, and chocolate functioned as currency, traded for favors or extra food. Skilled prisoners repaired boots, cut hair, or carved small crafts in exchange for supplies. Bartering created a fragile marketplace inside the wire, where survival often depended on negotiation rather than strength. In some camps, this informal economy became more organized than the official ration system.

88. Culture and Learning Behind Barbed Wire

Cultural life persisted even in confinement. Prisoners staged plays using makeshift costumes, formed choirs and bands, and organized lectures on history, mathematics, or languages. Former teachers held classes, determined that captivity would not steal years of learning. These activities were not luxuries but survival tools, helping men maintain routine and purpose when the future felt suspended indefinitely.

89. Discipline and Punishment in POW Camps

Discipline inside camps was usually strict but inconsistent. Minor rule-breaking could result in extra labor, confinement, or reduced rations, while serious offenses led to solitary cells or transfer to harsher facilities. Yet enforcement varied widely depending on guards and local commanders. Some camps were rigid and punitive, while others operated with surprising flexibility, reflecting how individual personalities often mattered more than official regulations.

90. Friendships Across Enemy Lines

Language barriers created unexpected challenges and alliances. Prisoners from different nations were sometimes housed together, forced to communicate through gestures, shared slang, or improvised mixtures of words. Over time, friendships formed across national lines as men discovered that captivity made former enemies share the same daily struggles. The war's divisions blurred inside the wire, replaced by a common identity as prisoners.

91. Improvised Medicine in Prison Camps

Medical care in camps was uneven but often improvised. Doctors who were themselves prisoners treated the sick using limited supplies, converting barracks into makeshift hospitals. Disease spread easily in crowded conditions, especially influenza and dysentery, yet professional skill sometimes made the difference between life and death. In some cases, enemy medical staff cooperated quietly to prevent outbreaks that could devastate both prisoners and guards.

92. The Psychological Burden of Waiting

Time passed strangely in captivity. Without battle rhythms or clear progress, days blended together into long stretches of waiting. Some prisoners scratched calendars into wood or walls to track the date, refusing to let months disappear unnoticed. Others stopped counting altogether, finding it easier not to measure how much of their lives had slipped away. The psychological weight of lost time became one of captivity's heaviest burdens.

93. The Long Journey Home After Captivity

When the war finally ended, release was rarely immediate or orderly. Transportation networks were damaged, governments disorganized, and millions of men needed to be moved across continents. Prisoners sometimes waited months after the armistice before trains or ships arrived. For many, freedom came slowly, in stages, marked not by celebration but by confusion and exhaustion as they tried to rebuild lives paused years earlier.

94. The Quiet Scars of Prisoner Life

For some former prisoners, captivity left deeper memories than combat itself. Years spent behind wire, separated from home and stripped of control, reshaped how they viewed authority and national loyalty. The war they remembered most clearly was not the charge across no man's land, but the long, quiet struggle to remain human in a place designed to hold them still.

EIGHT

Heroes, Legends & Life at the Front

While the history of the World War I is often told through the dates of battles and the names of generals, the true story lives in the remarkable experiences of the people who were there. This chapter looks at the human side of the conflict, from the famous figures who served in the mud before they became world leaders or legendary authors to the extraordinary bravery of units like the Harlem Hellfighters and the Lost Battalion. It also explores the smaller, everyday parts of life at the front, including the songs the soldiers sang, and the strange superstitions they relied on to get through each day. These are the legends and personal stories that show how, even in the middle of a global catastrophe, the human spirit found ways to endure, laugh, and hope.

95. The Lost Battalion in the Argonne Forest

In October 1918, deep in the tangled woods of France's Argonne Forest, more than 500 American soldiers advanced farther than anyone realized and accidentally marched straight into a trap. Thick trees, smoke, and confusion hid the enemy's movements, and by the time officers understood their position, German troops had already slipped around both flanks and sealed the gap behind them. The unit, made up mostly of the 77th Division from New York, suddenly found itself completely surrounded, cut off from supplies, reinforcements, and even its own army. Phone lines were severed by shellfire, runners sent for help were shot or captured, and food quickly ran out. The men dug shallow foxholes among the roots and rocks and prepared to hold their ground.

For nearly a week they endured constant attacks from every direction. Snipers fired from the trees. Artillery pounded their small pocket of forest day and night. Water grew scarce, rations dwindled to almost nothing, and the wounded piled up faster than medics could treat them. At one point, American artillery, unaware of their exact position, began shelling their own trapped troops. With no other way to communicate, the soldiers turned to carrier pigeons. One desperate note read, "Our artillery is dropping a barrage directly on us. For heaven's sake stop it." The message was tied to a pigeon named Cher Ami. Shot through the chest and losing a leg, the bird still flew miles through the gunfire and delivered the note, saving the survivors from being destroyed by friendly fire.

By the time relief forces finally broke through, nearly two-thirds of the battalion were dead, wounded, or missing. The men who staggered out of the forest looked skeletal, filthy, and half-starved, having survived for days on almost nothing while fighting off repeated assaults. Newspapers later called them "The Lost Battalion," turning their ordeal into a symbol of stubborn endurance.

96. From the Trenches to the Birth of Jazz in Europe

Among the American troops who arrived in France was the 369th Infantry Regiment, an all-Black unit from New York that would later earn the nickname "The Harlem Hellfighters." Because of segregation in the U.S. Army, they were often assigned labor duties instead of combat and were initially treated as second-class soldiers. But they brought something no other unit did: a full regimental band led by composer and conductor James Reese Europe. Packed with brass horns, clarinets, drums, and banjos, the band played a fast, syncopated style of music that many Europeans had never heard before, early jazz.

When the Hellfighters performed in French towns and behind the lines, crowds gathered instantly. Their music was louder, livelier, and freer than traditional military marches. Instead of stiff parades, people danced. Soldiers who had just come off the front forgot the war for a few minutes, clapping and laughing in muddy boots. The band toured constantly, sometimes playing for thousands at a time, introducing jazz to villages, cities, and even Parisian theaters. Many historians later credited them with helping spark Europe's first real exposure to jazz music.

The regiment itself also saw heavy combat, spending more days in the trenches than almost any other American unit and earning high praise from the French army, which awarded many of them the Croix de Guerre for bravery. Yet their cultural impact may have lasted even longer than their battlefield record. Long after the guns fell silent, the rhythms they carried overseas kept spreading.

97. A Pacifist Who Became a War Hero

Not every extraordinary moment of the war involved massive machines or entire divisions. Sometimes it came down to one exhausted soldier with a rifle. In October 1918, during the Meuse-Argonne Offensive, a quiet Tennessee farm boy named Alvin York found himself leading a small group of American troops through thick woods when they suddenly walked into a nest of German machine guns. The first burst of fire dropped most of the Americans instantly. Officers were killed, men scattered, and York, now one of the few still standing, suddenly found himself in charge.

Before the war, York had been a deeply religious pacifist who didn't even want to fight. He believed killing was wrong and had tried to claim conscientious objector status. Only after long conversations with his pastor did he reluctantly agree that defending others might be justified. Now, under fire, that decision was being tested. Instead of retreating, York crawled forward alone. Using a rifle and his skill as a hunter, he began picking off German gunners one by one with calm, careful shots. When a group charged him with bayonets, he switched to his pistol and dropped them at close range. The sudden, precise fire convinced many Germans that they were facing a much larger force. Confused and intimidated, dozens began surrendering.

By the end of the fight, York and a handful of surviving Americans had captured 132 German soldiers and silenced more than thirty machine guns almost single-handedly. What began as an ambush turned into one of the most unlikely reversals of the war. York later received the Medal of Honor and returned home to national fame, though he always downplayed the story, insisting he had simply done what he had to do.

98. The Attack of the Dead Men at Osowiec Fortress

One of the strangest and most nightmarish battles of the entire war took place at the Russian-held Osowiec Fortress in 1915, during a German gas attack so horrific that it later sounded more like legend than history. Before dawn, German artillery fired shells filled with chlorine gas, releasing a thick, greenish cloud that rolled slowly toward the Russian trenches like fog. Chlorine reacted with moisture in the lungs to form acid, burning throats and eyes, blistering skin, and drowning men from the inside as their lungs filled with fluid. Soldiers choked, vomited blood, and collapsed where they stood. Vegetation blackened, birds fell from the sky, and even metal equipment corroded in the fumes. From a distance, the fortress looked silent and dead. Convinced that no one could have survived, German infantry advanced confidently to occupy the position.

Then shapes began moving in the haze. Out of the drifting gas stumbled dozens of Russian survivors, barely alive but still armed. Their faces were wrapped in blood-soaked rags, uniforms torn and burned by chemicals, coughing up blood and pieces of lung tissue as they staggered forward. Some could barely stand. Others leaned on rifles like walking sticks. Yet instead of retreating, they charged. Witnesses later said the men looked like corpses clawing their way out of graves. Terrified by the sight of these half-blinded, half-suffocated figures screaming and advancing through the smoke, the German troops broke formation and fled in panic. The fortress held. The clash became known as "The Attack of the Dead Men," a moment when shock and fear proved stronger than gas or artillery, and when soldiers who should have been dead somehow kept fighting anyway.

99. The Hidden War Beneath the Trenches

Some soldiers didn't just live underground, they fought there. Along parts of the Western Front, specialist tunnelling units spent months digging secret passageways beneath enemy trenches, turning the war into a silent, suffocating world beneath the battlefield. Recruited mainly from coal miners, engineers, and railway workers who already knew how to work in tight spaces, these men carved tunnels by hand with picks and short shovels, scraping through clay and chalk while lying almost flat on their stomachs. Many shafts were barely three or four feet (about one meter) high, forcing men to crawl or crouch the entire time. The earth pressed in from all sides. Timber supports creaked constantly. Every few minutes, dirt trickled down from the ceiling like slow rain.

Light was scarce. Candles, oil lamps, or small carbide lamps gave off weak yellow glows and filled the air with smoke. Sometimes the flame would suddenly gutter out, a terrifying sign that oxygen was running low or gas had built up. The air smelled of damp soil, sweat, and stale breath. Ventilation was poor, and some tunnels grew so hot and stuffy that men struggled to breathe. There were no proper toilets, only buckets or tins shoved into corners, quickly turning the cramped passages foul. After hours underground, clothes were soaked with mud and grime, faces streaked black like coal miners.

Silence was everything. Even a dropped tool might give away their position. Many worked barefoot or in socks to muffle sound, stopping constantly to press their ears or stethoscopes against the walls to listen for enemy digging only feet away. If they broke through into an opposing tunnel, the fighting became desperate and primitive. There was no space to swing rifles, so men used pistols, bayonets, knives, clubs, or even sharpened entrenching tools in near-total darkness, grappling at arm's length in choking dust. The real objective was explosives. Tunnellers packed chambers with tons of ammonal beneath enemy lines, then retreated and detonated the charges, blowing entire trenches into the air like volcanoes. Some explosions were so massive they were heard dozens of miles away.

The work was so claustrophobic and nerve-racking that many veterans later said they feared the underground more than open combat. This hidden war beneath the trenches inspired modern portrayals like Thomas Shelby in *Peaky Blinders*, whose tunnelling scenes closely mirror the real experiences of these men. For them, the front line wasn't above ground at all, but in the dark earth itself, fighting an unseen enemy through inches of soil.

100. When Horses Beat Machine Guns

While most of World War I was fought from muddy trenches in Europe, one of its most dramatic battles took place thousands of miles away in the desert. After the failure of Gallipoli, Australian and New Zealand troops were redeployed to Egypt and the Middle East to protect the Suez Canal and fight the Ottoman Empire in what became the Sinai and Palestine Campaign. There, wide open terrain made horses useful again, and the Australian Light Horse became fast-moving desert fighters instead of trench soldiers.

On October 31, 1917, near the town of Beersheba, the Allies faced a desperate problem: water. Without capturing the town's wells before nightfall, thousands of men and horses risked collapsing from dehydration. With time running out, commanders ordered something almost unthinkable in modern warfare, a full cavalry charge straight at entrenched defenders.

Just before sunset, nearly 800 riders formed up in long ranks. Bayonets were held in their hands like makeshift swords, since they carried no traditional sabers. Then the order came. The horses surged forward at a trot, then a gallop, hooves thundering across the hard desert floor. Dust clouds rose behind them as Turkish artillery and machine guns opened fire. Shells burst overhead, bullets kicked up sand, but the riders kept coming, faster and faster.

The speed saved them. Enemy gunners had trouble lowering their sights quickly enough to hit targets moving so fast. Within minutes, the Australians were crashing over the trenches, leaping obstacles, and fighting hand-to-hand among stunned defenders who had expected an infantry assault, not a wall of charging horses. By nightfall, Beersheba was captured, along with its precious wells, and the advance continued.

The charge cost dozens of lives, but it succeeded where slower tactics might have failed. For many Australians and New Zealanders, it became a symbol of daring, improvisation, and "mateship" under pressure. Photographs of mounted troops racing across open desert stand in sharp contrast to the barbed wire and mud of the Western Front.

101. Marks Left in the Trenches

The walls of trenches, dugouts, and ruined buildings slowly filled with graffiti as soldiers carved their presence into the war wherever they could. Men scratched their names, hometowns, and dates into wooden beams and chalky stone, leaving behind simple lines like "Tom, Manchester, 1916" or "Still here somehow." Others posted dark jokes and warnings, painting signs that read "If you're reading this, you're too tall" near sniper zones or "Keep your head down" above exposed corners. Directions were mocked with arrows pointing "This way to Berlin," while miserable sectors earned sarcastic welcomes such as "Hotel Somme" or "Paradise Alley." Rotating units left messages for the next group: "Good luck lads" or "Watch the rats at night," turning the trenches into a kind of passing conversation between strangers. Long after the fighting stopped, archaeologists and hikers would still find these carvings preserved in concrete and wood, small handwritten proof that frightened young men had once stood there, trying to leave some trace that they had existed at all.

102. The Dark Humor of Trench Songs

Songs became one of the fastest ways trench slang, complaints, and dark humor spread across the front, with soldiers constantly rewriting familiar tunes to match their reality. Cheerful prewar music hall songs were often sung with heavy irony, like *"Pack Up Your Troubles in Your Old Kit-Bag, and smile, smile, smile,"* belted out while men marched through rain and mud with anything but smiles. Others were openly sarcastic, such as the endlessly repeated chant set to *Auld Lang Syne*: *"We're here because we're here, because we're here, because we're here,"* a deliberately pointless lyric that joked about the senselessness of their situation. Some songs mocked officers directly, especially in the popular trench parody *"Hanging on the Old Barbed Wire,"* where verses complained, *"If you want to find the general, I know where he is… he's hanging on the old barbed wire,"* a biting joke about leaders staying safely behind the lines. Men sang while marching, digging, or waiting for rations, passing verses from unit to unit until entire battalions knew the same choruses. In a world of shellfire and orders, these songs became a shared language of sarcasm and survival, turning fear and frustration into something you could shout together in the dark.

103. Code Words Soldiers Used for War

Soldiers also developed a quiet system of code words and euphemisms that allowed them to talk about danger without ever naming it directly. Instead of saying an attack, they might casually mention "going over for a stroll" or "doing a bit of work tonight," while a hazardous repair mission became a harmless-sounding "working party." Dawn and dusk alerts were simply "stand-to," and a supposedly safe stretch of line was labeled a "quiet sector," a phrase veterans learned to distrust immediately. Death itself was softened into phrases like "lost," "missing," or "not coming back," and being sent away sick or injured was described as "getting a ticket out." Officers wrote reports filled with bland wording such as "slight losses" or "enemy activity," language that hid the chaos underneath. Over time, this understatement became second nature, turning catastrophe into routine vocabulary. By shrinking terrifying events into mild phrases, soldiers protected themselves emotionally, speaking about the worst moments of their lives as if they were nothing more than minor inconveniences.

104. From Trenches to Everyday Speech

World War I didn't just redraw maps and topple empires. It quietly rewired everyday language. Words that had once belonged strictly to generals and field reports slipped into kitchens, classrooms, and shop floors. Civilians reading newspapers suddenly spoke of the "front line," "mobilizing," "casualties," and "barrages" as casually as weather forecasts. War vocabulary became normal vocabulary. Conflict, urgency, and even business problems were described using the language of battle, as if the entire world had begun thinking like an army.

At the same time, the men actually living in the trenches invented a private dialect to survive mentally as much as physically. The front was too miserable to describe plainly, so everything was renamed with dry humor. A tiny dirt shelter scraped into a wall became a "funk hole." Wooden planks over the mud were "duckboards." Tins of corned beef were "bully beef," hard crackers "dog biscuits," and lice "chats," leading to the daily ritual of "chatting" for hours while picking them out of seams. Big shells were "whizz-bangs" or "Jack Johnsons," nicknamed after the heavyweight boxer because they hit with a crushing punch. A safer posting was "cushy." Dawn and dusk alerts were simply "stand-to." The vocabulary made chaos sound domestic, almost ordinary, as if renaming danger could shrink it.

Humor went further. Shellfire was described as "a bit lively." Flooded trenches became "the seaside." Rats were "trench terriers." Death itself softened into phrases like "gone west." Even letters home were coded. Because officers might read every line, soldiers learned to understate everything. A bombardment became "busy today." A coming assault was "going for a walk." A miserable, rat-infested hole was "comfortable enough." Families learned that cheerful phrases usually meant the opposite. This habit of understatement followed many veterans home, shaping a restrained, guarded way of speaking long after the guns fell silent.

The trenches were also linguistic melting pots. British troops longed for "Blighty," their slang for home, and called a lucky wound a "Blighty one" if it meant evacuation. Australians spoke of their "mates" and cursed foolish officers as "drongos." Canadians mixed British and American expressions like "buddy" and "okay." Indian soldiers shared words like "pukka" for something genuine and "dekko" for a quick look. African troops contributed terms such as "askari" and "safari." In crowded dugouts and marching columns, these phrases spread from unit to unit, turning the front into an accidental classroom where words traveled faster than any official language ever could.

Even the need for speed changed speech. Expressions like "AWOL" (absent without leave) and "SNAFU" (situation normal, all fouled up) grew from the need to convey complex situations quickly under stress. Wartime communication favored short, efficient language that later influenced everything from offices to government paperwork.

When the war ended, the vocabulary didn't stay behind. Veterans carried it into civilian life, and soon factories launched "campaigns," politicians planned "offensives," newspapers covered elections like "battles," and workers complained about being "in the trenches." Sports teams "attacked" and "defended." Without realizing it, society kept speaking the language of war. The mud and barbed wire were gone, but the words remained, shaping how an entire generation described effort, struggle, and loss. In that sense, World War I never fully ended. It lived on every time someone said they were holding the line.

105. Brilliant Minds in the Shadow of War

Not everyone who shaped the twentieth century carried a rifle the same way, and the war pulled brilliant minds into it from every direction, some into uniform, others into open protest. In Britain, philosopher Bertrand Russell refused to fight at all. While patriotic crowds cheered enlistment, Russell publicly condemned the war as a tragic mistake driven by nationalism, pride, and political ego. He gave speeches against conscription, wrote essays attacking the government, and urged young men not to sacrifice themselves for what he believed was pointless slaughter. Authorities treated dissent almost like treason. He lost his lectureship at Cambridge, was fined, banned from certain cities, and in 1918 was jailed for months. From his prison cell he continued writing about peace, free speech, and civil liberties, becoming one of the most famous antiwar voices of the era. Simply questioning the war could cost a man his job, reputation, and freedom.

At the same time, millions of other young men who would later become household names were quietly serving in the mud like everyone else. J.R.R. Tolkien worked as a signals officer at the Somme, watching most of his closest friends die, experiences that later echoed in the bleak landscapes, loyal friendships, and sense of loss that filled The Lord of the Rings. Adolf Hitler served as a German messenger, running through shellfire with dispatches and earning medals for bravery, wounds and defeat feeding the bitterness and nationalism that later defined his politics. Future U.S. President Harry Truman commanded an artillery battery in France and learned leadership under fire. Ernest Hemingway drove ambulances for the Red Cross, was badly wounded by mortar fire, and later turned those memories into A Farewell to Arms. Walt Disney, still underage, lied about his age to enlist as an ambulance driver and decorated his vehicle with cartoons to amuse wounded soldiers. Even A. A. Milne, creator of Winnie-the-Pooh, first wore a British officer's uniform in the trenches.

106. Christmas in the Trenches

Even in the middle of war, the calendar still turned, and Christmas became one of the few moments when the trenches briefly felt human again. In December, parcels from home increased, stuffed with fruitcake, chocolate, socks, scarves, tobacco, and small gifts that were saved carefully for the day itself. Units decorated dugouts with scraps of greenery, empty shell casings, or candles stuck into bottles to resemble makeshift trees. Cooks improvised special meals when supplies allowed, adding extra meat, jam, or pudding to rations, and tea or rum was issued more generously than usual. Men sang carols softly at night, shared food between platoons, and wrote longer letters home describing the strange mix of celebration and homesickness. In quieter sectors, football matches, concerts, or small church services were organized behind the lines.

The most famous Christmas came in 1914, when parts of the Western Front fell unexpectedly silent in what became known as the Christmas Truce. It was not ordered by generals or planned by politicians but began spontaneously when German soldiers placed small Christmas trees and candles along their parapets and started singing carols like *Stille Nacht (Silent Night)* across the darkness. British troops answered with songs of their own, and soon voices replaced rifle fire. Curious men cautiously climbed out of their trenches, meeting halfway in no man's land with raised hands and nervous smiles. They shook hands, exchanged cigarettes, chocolate, buttons, and caps, and helped one another bury bodies that had been lying between the lines for weeks. In some places they posed for photographs together or kicked footballs back and forth in the mud. The truce lasted only hours in some sectors and a day or two in others before officers ordered everyone back to their positions and the shooting slowly resumed. Still, for a brief moment, the war loosened its grip, and enemies saw each other not as targets but as ordinary young men far from home, sharing the same cold and longing for peace.

107. The Rituals Soldiers Used to Cheat Fate

In a war where death often felt random and unpredictable, many soldiers clung to small superstitions and lucky charms, believing that tiny rituals might somehow tilt fate in their favor. Coins, lockets, photographs, or scraps of ribbon from sweethearts were tucked into breast pockets like protective talismans. Some men carried rabbit's feet, church medals, or bits of hometown soil sewn into their uniforms. Others refused to change "lucky" socks, wore the same scarf on every patrol, or insisted on stepping into the trench with the same foot first each morning. Dice, playing cards, and carved trinkets became pocket charms rubbed before going over the top. Entire units developed shared rituals, avoiding certain dugouts considered unlucky or repeating the same jokes and phrases before attacks. Even hardened veterans who claimed not to believe often followed these habits quietly, reasoning that it was safer not to tempt fate. In a world ruled by artillery and chance, these small objects and routines offered something the war rarely did, the comforting illusion of control.

NINE

The War at Home

World War I was not just fought on distant battlefields; it was a conflict that reached into every home, factory, and street across the globe. As the struggle dragged on, the line between the soldier and the civilian began to disappear, and the people left behind were called upon to support the war effort in ways never seen before. This chapter looks at the reality of life on the home front, from the massive social changes that saw women entering the industrial workforce to the clever and often intense ways that governments used propaganda and rationing to keep their nations focused on the fight. It was a time of shared sacrifice and immense pressure, where the endurance of those at home became just as vital to the final outcome as the strength of the armies at the front.

108. The Birth of Total War

When the war erupted in 1914, almost everyone believed it would be short. Politicians spoke confidently of being "home by Christmas." Generals expected a few decisive battles followed by peace talks. Factories continued making consumer goods, shops stayed open, and most civilians assumed the fighting would be handled by professional soldiers far away. But within months, the reality shattered those expectations. The front lines barely moved, casualties climbed into the hundreds of thousands, and armies burned through ammunition, food, uniforms, and fuel at a pace no peacetime economy had ever imagined. The war wasn't ending. It was expanding.

Governments quickly realized something alarming: the battlefield wasn't just short of men, it was short of everything. Guns needed shells. Soldiers needed boots. Railways needed coal. Hospitals needed bandages. Every day the front consumed mountains of supplies that had to be replaced immediately or entire offensives would stall. Victory no longer depended only on bravery or tactics. It depended on production. So states did something unprecedented. They stepped in and took control.

Factories that had once competed freely were reorganized like military units. Car plants stopped making cars and began building trucks, ambulances, and aircraft parts. Piano makers produced shell casings. Bicycle shops machined rifle components. Textile mills churned out uniforms and bandages instead of clothing. Steelworks forged artillery barrels around the clock. Governments created powerful ministries (like Britain's Ministry of Munitions) that told businesses exactly what to produce and how much. Quotas replaced profits. Output charts replaced sales targets. Whistles and sirens marked shifts like bugles marked drills.

Civilians were mobilized almost like soldiers. Millions of men left farms and offices for the trenches, and women filled their places in factories and transport jobs. Children collected scrap metal. Families planted vegetable gardens to stretch food supplies. Coal, rubber, and bread were rationed. Railways prioritized troop trains over passengers.

By 1915, it was clear this was no longer a conflict between armies. It was a contest between whole societies. One side's strength came not just from its generals, but from how many shells its factories could produce, how much food its farms could grow, and how long its civilians could endure shortages and long shifts. The war had spread far beyond the trenches. It had reached into workshops, kitchens, and city streets, turning entire nations into vast, coordinated war machines. For the first time in history, everyone was part of the front line.

109. The Women Who Powered the War

When millions of men marched off to war, their places at the machines could not stay empty. By 1915–16, governments realized that winning battles depended just as much on shells and bullets as on soldiers. So the gates of heavy industry swung open to women for the first time. Across Britain, France, Germany, and beyond, women poured into shipyards, steel mills, and especially munitions factories, trading aprons and classrooms for overalls, gloves, and steel presses. In Britain alone, more than a million women entered munitions work, and by the middle of the war women made up the majority of workers producing shells, cartridges, and explosives.

The work was exhausting and relentless. Shifts often lasted 10–12 hours, sometimes longer during offensives when armies demanded millions of extra rounds. Factories ran day and night under bright electric lamps, machines pounding without pause. Women stood for hours filling shells with TNT, screwing in fuses, polishing brass casings, hauling crates, or operating heavy lathes and presses that shook the floor. Supervisors treated output like a battlefield objective. Every delay meant fewer shells at the front.

But the real danger wasn't just fatigue. It was the chemicals. TNT dust soaked into hair, clothes, and skin. Over time it stained workers a sickly yellow color and irritated their eyes and lungs. Their faces, hands, and even the whites of their eyes could turn mustard-yellow, earning them the nickname "canary girls." Some suffered headaches, nausea, liver damage, or poisoning. A few collapsed at their benches. Yet many kept working because the pay, though still unequal, was often better than anything they had earned before.

Explosions were an ever-present fear. Entire buildings could vanish in a second if sparks hit loose powder. In several disasters, factories detonated with the force of small earthquakes, killing dozens or even hundreds at once. Windows shattered miles away. Roofs lifted into the sky. Rescue crews sometimes found nothing but craters where workshops had stood. Unlike the trenches, there were no medals or parades here, yet these women were dying in what many quietly called the "factory front line."

Still, for many, the job brought something new and unexpected: independence. Regular wages meant their own money, their own choices. Some rented rooms, bought bicycles, went to cinemas, or supported families without relying on husbands or fathers. For the first time, women handled heavy machinery, worked in teams, joined unions, and proved they could do jobs once declared impossible for them.

When the war ended, many were pushed back out of these roles to make space for returning men. But the change couldn't be fully undone. The experience had cracked open old assumptions. Women had built the shells, forged the steel, and kept the war running. After proving they could power an entire industrial nation, it was much harder to argue they belonged only in kitchens and parlors. The factories had quietly reshaped society as surely as the trenches had reshaped the battlefield.

110. Wages, Coins, and Independence

Money itself felt different during the war, partly because the old British currency system sounded like a code. Instead of simple dollars and cents, pay was counted in pounds, shillings, and pence. One pound (£1) equaled 20 shillings, and one shilling equaled 12 pence, meaning there were 240 pence in a pound. A few coins could still buy everyday necessities. A loaf of bread might cost 1–2 pence, a tram ride a penny, and weekly rent for a small room perhaps 5–8 shillings. A cinema ticket was often just 3–6 pence, cheap enough for an evening out after work. A sturdy pair of leather boots might cost 6–10 shillings, a winter coat around a pound, and a second-hand bicycle, one of the most desired symbols of independence, could be bought for £3–£5, letting a woman travel miles without relying on trams or escorts. Small luxuries suddenly felt possible: tea in a café, a new hat, a gramophone record, or a few shillings sent home to family each week. Motorcars technically existed, but they were still luxury items costing £150 or more, far beyond a factory worker's reach and mostly owned by doctors, businessmen, or the wealthy. For most women, the bicycle, not the car, was the true vehicle of freedom, turning wages into mobility and independence in a way earlier generations had never experienced. So even what looks like a small number on paper could stretch surprisingly far.

Before the war, many working-class women earned very little actual cash. Domestic servants, shop girls, laundresses, or farm hands often made only 10–15 shillings a week. Some were partly paid in food and lodging rather than wages. In modern terms, that might equal roughly $80–$120 a week today, barely enough for independence. Many handed their pay straight to parents or husbands and kept almost nothing themselves.

War industry changed their earning power dramatically. Women in munitions and engineering plants commonly earned 30–40 shillings a week, and with overtime or skilled tasks some reached 50–60 shillings. That was double or triple their old income. Converted to today's money, this might look like about $250–$350 a week, or roughly $1,000–$1,400 a month. By modern standards that sounds modest, but at 1916 prices it could cover rent, food, coal for heating, clothes, and still leave savings. For many women, it was the first time they had steady disposable income at all.

Payday became a small ceremony. Wages were often handed out in envelopes of coins and notes on Friday afternoons. Women counted their money right there on the factory floor, comparing totals, planning purchases, sending a few shillings home, or saving for boots, a bicycle, or a cinema ticket. Diaries mention the quiet pride of buying things without asking permission from anyone.

111. Factories Ordered to War

As the war dragged on and casualties mounted, governments realized that victory would depend not just on soldiers, but on production. In 1915 Britain created the Ministry of Munitions, a powerful new department that effectively took control of large parts of the economy and began running industry like an army. Private businesses no longer chose what they made or how much. Instead, telegrams and official orders arrived with exact instructions: convert your workshop, retool your machines, produce this many shells by this date. Car factories that once built touring cars were ordered to manufacture artillery shells and engines. Piano makers, skilled at bending wood and shaping metal frames, were reassigned to make shell casings. Bicycle shops began producing gun parts and ball bearings. Even small family workshops found themselves suddenly making fuses, detonators, or rifle components.

Production targets were strict and mathematical. A plant might be told to deliver 10,000 shells per week, 50 machine guns per month, or thousands of rifles by a fixed deadline. Inspectors checked output constantly. If a factory fell short, managers could be fined, removed, or even threatened with government takeover. Workers were sometimes forbidden to leave their jobs, and strikes in key industries were restricted or temporarily banned under wartime laws. Yet these were not unpaid demands. The government issued formal contracts and paid companies directly, often guaranteeing profits to keep production flowing, turning war work into a massive state-funded enterprise.

For the first time in modern history, an entire industrial nation functioned under centralized command. Schedules, quotas, and supply chains were treated like military orders. Steel, coal, and labor were allocated the way generals allocated troops. Factories became regiments, foremen acted like officers, and output numbers were measured almost like battlefield victories.

112. When the Guns Ran Out of Ammunition

By 1915, the First World War had already revealed a brutal truth: modern war consumed ammunition faster than any nation on earth could manufacture it. Prewar planners had imagined short campaigns lasting weeks. Instead, guns fired for months without pause. On some days, a single British artillery battery might fire more shells in an hour than entire armies had used in previous wars. During major offensives, thousands of guns firing together could burn through hundreds of thousands of shells in a single day. Entire hillsides shook continuously, and ammunition trains struggled to keep up. Then, suddenly, the impossible happened: the shells ran out.

This shortage became known as the "Shell Crisis" of 1915–16. British units preparing for attacks discovered their guns had only a few days' supply left. Some batteries were ordered to fire sparingly, rationing shots as if counting food. Infantry assaults went forward without proper bombardments, costing thousands of lives because enemy barbed wire and machine-gun nests remained intact. Newspapers exploded with anger, blaming the government for sending men into battle without bullets. It was one of the first moments civilians realized the war wasn't just fought by soldiers, but by factories.

The solution required something unprecedented: entire economies were reorganized for total war. Governments seized control of industry, creating ministries of munitions and converting anything that could hold a lathe (a machine tool that shapes metal by spinning the material very fast while a cutting blade shaves pieces off) into a weapons factory. Car plants, sewing machine workshops, piano makers, and bicycle companies suddenly found themselves producing rifles, shells, and machine-gun parts. Women flooded into these factories by the hundreds of thousands, operating presses and packing explosives around the clock. In Britain alone, shell production jumped from roughly 13,000 shells per day in 1914 to over 1.5 million per day by 1916. By the end of the war, millions of shells were being produced every single week.

Making a single artillery shell wasn't simple. Steel had to be forged and machined precisely, packed with high explosives, fitted with fuses, painted, inspected, and transported. A heavy shell could take hours of labor across multiple factories before it ever reached the front. Rifles required dozens of parts milled to tight tolerances. Tanks, still new and experimental, took weeks to assemble, involving engines, armor plates, tracks, and crews of specialized workers. Costs soared into billions. A single artillery shell might equal hundreds of dollars in modern money. Multiply that by millions fired each month, and the scale became staggering.

By 1917–18, the war had become less a contest of generals and more a contest of production lines. Victory depended not only on courage, but on which nation could manufacture more steel, more explosives, and more bullets faster than the other side. In the trenches, soldiers experienced war one shot at a time. Behind the lines, entire cities roared day and night to keep those shots coming, proving that modern warfare wasn't just fought at the front, but hammered, welded, and packed in factories miles away.

113. Turning Junk into Weapons

As the war dragged on and artillery consumed steel faster than mines and factories could replace it, governments began asking civilians for something unexpected: their junk. Old metal suddenly became as valuable as ammunition. Towns across Britain, France, Germany, and the United States organized massive scrap metal drives, urging families to donate anything made of iron, brass, copper, or steel so it could be melted down and turned into shells, rifles, rails, and machine parts.

Posters declared that "Every pound of metal is a bullet" or "Your old pot could save a soldier." Schoolchildren collected nails and hinges. Housewives gave up kettles, pans, and broken stoves. Churches donated cracked bells. Parks lost their decorative railings. Iron fences, gates, bed frames, farm tools, plumbing pipes, and even statues disappeared onto carts headed for foundries. In some cities, entire lampposts and tram tracks were removed and replaced with cheaper wood or concrete.

The numbers were staggering. Single cities sometimes gathered thousands of tons in a few weeks, enough metal to produce millions of artillery shells. Trains hauled scrap to giant steelworks where it was sorted, melted in roaring furnaces, and poured into molds for new weapons. Yesterday's frying pan might return to the front as a shell casing within days.

For civilians, it made the war feel uncomfortably close. Streets literally changed shape. Homes grew barer. Everyday life looked stripped and temporary. Children grew up playing in parks without fences because the metal had gone to the front.

114. When Every Meal Was Measured

As the war tightened its grip on shipping and farmland, food quietly became another battlefield. German submarines sank merchant ships faster than Britain could replace them, and by 1917 the country was importing barely half the grain and meat it normally relied on. Store shelves thinned, queues stretched around corners, and panic buying emptied shops within hours. To prevent hunger and riots, the government stepped in and began regulating what every household could eat.

By the later years of the war, many adults lived on strict weekly rations that sounded small even on paper: about 1 pound (450 grams) of meat, 8 ounces (225 grams) of sugar, 4 ounces (115 grams) of butter or margarine, 4 ounces (115 grams) of bacon or ham, and just 2 ounces (55 grams) of tea. Bread was sometimes limited or stretched with cheaper flours. Those amounts weren't daily allowances, they were for an entire week. A pound of meat had to last seven days. Sugar worked out to barely two spoonfuls a day. Butter became something you scraped thinly, not spread. Eggs were scarce luxuries. Milk was prioritized for children and the sick. Coal, needed for cooking and heating, was also rationed, meaning families often had to choose between a hot meal or a warm room.

Prices were tightly controlled to stop profiteering. Bread, milk, and coal were capped at fixed costs so the poor wouldn't be priced out of survival. Shopkeepers who overcharged could be fined or shut down. Even so, people grew used to substitutes and stretching meals. Margarine replaced butter. Turnips and potatoes bulked out stews. Bones were boiled repeatedly for soup. Tea leaves were reused until they turned pale.

To fill the gap, civilians were urged to grow their own food. Parks, schoolyards, and back gardens were turned into "victory gardens," rows of cabbages, carrots, and beans planted wherever there was soil. Children kept chickens. Office workers dug potatoes after work. Posters urged people to "Dig for Victory" and waste nothing. Saving leftovers became patriotic, almost like conserving ammunition.

By the end of the war, the average dinner table looked very different from the one people remembered in 1914. Meals were smaller, plainer, and carefully measured.

115. When the Fields Replaced the Classroom

As millions of adult men left farms for the army, the countryside suddenly faced a different kind of emergency: there was no one left to grow food. Crops still needed planting, harvesting, and hauling, but the strongest workers were now in uniform somewhere in France. To keep the nation fed, governments quietly turned to the people who were still available; women, the elderly, and children. Across Britain and much of Europe, schoolboys and girls as young as twelve or thirteen were pulled from classrooms and sent into the fields to replace missing laborers.

At first it was presented as patriotic volunteer work, but it quickly became organized and semi-compulsory. Schools shortened terms or closed entirely during harvest seasons. Teachers marched groups of children out to farms where they weeded rows, picked potatoes, milked cows, scared birds from grain, and hauled heavy sacks that sometimes weighed nearly as much as they did. Some worked ten-hour days in mud and rain for only a few pennies. Others lived temporarily on farms in rough dormitories, sleeping in barns or sheds. Blisters, backaches, and exhaustion became normal parts of childhood.

Britain even created official programs like the School Harvest Camps and later the Women's Land Army, where teenagers often worked alongside adult women, driving horses, operating tools, and performing jobs once considered strictly "men's work." Posters framed it as service equal to soldiering: "Food is Ammunition - Don't Waste It." Growing wheat or digging potatoes was treated almost like loading shells.

For many children, the war years meant fewer lessons and more labor. Some missed months of schooling. Others never fully returned. Yet their work mattered. Without those extra hands, cities already strained by submarine blockades and rationing might have faced real famine.

116. How World War I Shifted the Clock

One of the strangest "weapons" introduced during the war wasn't a gun or a shell, but the clock itself. By 1916, coal shortages were becoming serious across Europe. Coal powered everything: trains, factories, ships, electric lights, and home heating. Every extra hour of artificial light burned more fuel the war desperately needed for munitions and transport. So governments looked for a simple solution that cost nothing and saved millions of tons of energy. Their answer was to change time.

In the spring of 1916, Germany became the first country to introduce daylight saving time, moving clocks forward one hour so people would wake earlier and make better use of natural daylight. Britain followed within weeks, along with France and many other nations. The idea was straightforward: if sunset came "later" on the clock, families would use fewer lamps at night, factories could run longer on daylight, and less coal would be burned for lighting and heating.

The savings added up quickly. Officials estimated that Britain alone conserved hundreds of thousands of tons of coal per year, simply by shifting the clock. For a nation running railways, shipyards, and shell factories nonstop, that fuel meant more trains moving troops, more steel smelted, and more shells produced.

But the change felt strange at first. Farmers complained their animals didn't understand the new time. Children walked to school in darker mornings. Factory whistles blew "earlier" than they ever had. Newspapers printed guides explaining how to reset watches and clocks. Some people even feared it was government overreach, tampering with something as natural as time itself.

Still, the system worked well enough that it stuck. What began as an emergency wartime fuel-saving measure eventually became permanent policy in many countries. More than a century later, millions of people still change their clocks every spring and autumn, rarely realizing the habit started not for convenience, but because World War I turned even daylight into a resource to be rationed.

117. How Air Raids Changed City Nights

For the first time in history, civilians learned that war could arrive from the sky. Beginning in 1915, huge German Zeppelins (hydrogen-filled airships hundreds of feet long) drifted silently over the North Sea and dropped bombs on British towns and cities at night. They weren't very accurate, but accuracy didn't matter. From thousands of feet up, crews simply released explosives and incendiaries onto the glow of streetlights below. Entire neighborhoods suddenly realized that light itself had become a target.

The solution was something completely new: blackouts. When air raid warnings sounded, cities went dark within minutes. Streetlamps were switched off. Shop signs went black. Trams stopped running. Homes covered windows with thick curtains, blankets, or painted glass so no light leaked outside. Even a thin crack of yellow glow could attract bombs.

Police and volunteer wardens patrolled streets shouting at anyone who showed a candle or cigarette near a window.

Nighttime cities became eerie and silent. People stumbled through pitch-black streets, bumping into curbs and lampposts. Carriages and early cars crept forward without headlights or used tiny slits of light pointed downward. The sky overhead, once dotted with lamps and cafés, turned completely black except for searchlights and anti-aircraft flashes.

Factories and rail yards (prime targets) were especially strict. Workers sometimes finished shifts in total darkness to avoid revealing their position. The psychological effect was enormous. Children slept in basements. Families kept bags packed in case of evacuation.

Though later wars would perfect the system, World War I created the first true "lights out" cities, where millions of people learned that survival sometimes meant simply disappearing into the night.

118. The Strikes on the Factory Front

As the war dragged into its second and third years, the factories that fed the front began to resemble battlefields of their own. Munitions plants ran day and night under glaring lamps, machines clattering without pause, air thick with metal dust and chemical fumes. Shifts regularly stretched to ten, twelve, even fourteen hours, six or seven days a week. Overtime became normal. Sleep became rare. Many workers, especially women in shell and explosive plants, stood for hours at heavy presses or handled toxic chemicals that stained skin yellow and burned their lungs. Exhaustion built quietly, then snapped.

Despite patriotic posters urging everyone to "work as soldiers of industry," strikes still broke out. Workers walked off the job over low pay, unsafe conditions, food shortages, or simply sheer fatigue. In Britain alone, hundreds of small stoppages erupted between 1915 and 1918. Some lasted hours, others days. Entire factories sometimes shut down when thousands refused to clock in. It shocked the government: the same factories producing the shells and bullets needed at the front were suddenly silent.

The state reacted quickly and harshly. Under laws like the Munitions of War Act (1915), strikes were technically illegal. Workers were forbidden to leave their jobs without permission, wages were tightly controlled, and disputes were sent to compulsory arbitration. Skilled workers couldn't even change employers freely. In extreme cases, men who stopped work could be fined, arrested, or threatened with conscription into the army. Soldiers were occasionally stationed outside plants to keep order, a reminder that these "civilian" workplaces were now treated almost like military bases.

Yet the strikes never fully disappeared. Many were short "down tools" protests rather than full rebellions, brief acts of defiance to demand better hours or safer conditions. Sometimes they worked. Pay was raised. Shifts shortened slightly. Safety rules improved. The government realized that pushing workers too hard could stop production entirely.

The irony was unavoidable. While soldiers collapsed from shellfire at the front, workers collapsed from exhaustion at the machines behind it. Both were fighting the same war, just in different uniforms.

119. The Deadly Risks of Making Shells

Working in a munitions factory could be almost as dangerous as serving in the trenches. Explosives like TNT, cordite, and picric acid were packed, pressed, and poured by hand in huge quantities, often inside crowded wooden buildings designed for speed rather than safety. Floors were swept constantly to prevent sparks. Workers wore soft shoes with no nails. Metal tools were banned. Even a dropped hammer, a static shock, or a grain of dust in the wrong place could trigger a chain reaction. Everyone knew the rule: one mistake could erase the entire building. And sometimes it did.

On January 19, 1917, the Silvertown explosion in East London proved just how fragile these factories were. A plant refining TNT caught fire and then detonated with the force of a small earthquake. The blast was so powerful it shattered windows up to 10 miles (16 km) away and was heard across the city. Entire streets collapsed. Houses lifted off their foundations. Nearly 70,000 buildings were damaged, and the shockwave felt like an air raid. About 70 people were killed and hundreds injured, many of them ordinary civilians who had nothing to do with the factory but simply lived nearby. Survivors described a black cloud rising over London like a volcano.

Silvertown wasn't unique. Smaller explosions happened regularly across Britain, France, Germany, and the United States. Shell-filling plants sometimes erupted without warning, killing dozens or even hundreds in seconds. Newspapers occasionally downplayed the disasters to avoid hurting morale, but workers knew the risks. Some joked grimly that every shift might be their last.

Inside the plants, accidents were often sudden and invisible. A tray of unstable shells could detonate and set off the entire room. A spark in a cordite-drying shed could blow apart the roof. TNT dust in the air could ignite like gunpowder. When it happened, there was usually no escape. Entire sections simply vanished in flame.

Yet production rarely stopped for long. Debris was cleared, new sheds built, and workers returned within days. Replacement crews filled the gaps. The war demanded shells faster than safety improvements could keep up.

120. How War Bonds Funded the Fighting

World War I wasn't just fought with rifles and shells. It was fought with savings accounts. Modern industrial war cost so much money that taxes alone couldn't pay for it, so governments turned to their own citizens and essentially asked them to bankroll the fighting. Instead of forcing the money outright, they sold "War Bonds," loans from ordinary families to the state. Posters covered walls and train stations with slogans like "Lend Your Savings to Win the War," "Your Money Fights," and "Buy a Bond, Save a Soldier." Schoolchildren collected coins. Bank clerks encouraged customers to invest. Employers deducted bond payments directly from wages. The message was simple: even if you couldn't fight, your money could.

In Britain, the most famous was the 5% War Loan, which paid 5% interest each year. That meant if you lent the government £100, you earned £5 annually in return, a strong rate for the time. The bonds were marketed as both patriotic and practical, safe investments backed by the government itself. Families poured in life savings, shopkeepers invested profits, and entire communities subscribed together. By the end of the war, millions of citizens had become creditors to their own country.

The sums were staggering. Britain raised billions of pounds through bond drives, equivalent to hundreds of billions today. The war was literally financed by bakers, factory girls, teachers, and clerks. In some households, the bond certificate was treated like a family treasure, tucked into drawers beside birth certificates and wills.

But there was a catch: the money wasn't returned quickly. Some bonds weren't fully repaid for decades. In fact, portions of Britain's World War I debt weren't finally paid off until the 21st century. A grandmother's wartime investment could still be earning interest long after the trenches were gone.

For many civilians, buying a bond felt like sending a piece of themselves to the front. If their son couldn't be there, their savings would be. In that sense, the war didn't just mobilize soldiers and factories. It mobilized wallets. Entire nations were fighting not only with blood, but with borrowed money.

121. The Images That Drove the War Effort

Before the war, advertising sold soap and cigarettes. During the war, it sold survival. Governments plastered every wall, train station, and shop window with posters designed to tug at pride, fear, guilt, and duty. Bright colors, bold fonts, and simple slogans turned the entire country into one giant message board. Propaganda wasn't subtle. It pointed fingers, shamed hesitation, and reminded people daily that the war depended on them personally.

One of the most famous images showed Britain's war secretary, Lord Kitchener, staring straight at the viewer with his finger extended: "Your Country Needs YOU." The design was so powerful it was copied worldwide, including America's Uncle Sam poster. Another showed women and children waving goodbye under the words "Women of Britain Say — GO!", implying that real men enlisted and that families expected it. Some posters went further, showing little girls asking their fathers, "Daddy, what did YOU do in the Great War?" quietly threatening future shame for anyone who stayed home.

Factories displayed signs reading "Every Shell Saves Lives" or "Speed Means Victory." Newspapers printed stories of enemy "atrocities," sometimes exaggerated or invented, to keep anger high and doubt low. Germans were often portrayed as monsters or apes, making the conflict feel moral as well as military.

Politicians reinforced it with speeches. British Prime Minister David Lloyd George spoke of fighting "a war to end war" and insisted the nation must mobilize "every man and every woman, every shilling and every resource." The language made factories sound like battlefields and workers sound like soldiers. Even children collected scrap metal and knitted socks because they were told they were part of the fight. By 1918, propaganda shaped daily life so completely that it was hard to separate reality from messaging. It filled streets, classrooms, pay packets, and newspapers.

TEN

A Global Conflict

World War I is often remembered through the lens of the Western Front, but the reality is that the conflict stretched across every continent and ocean on the planet. From the deserts of the Middle East to the jungles of Africa and the islands of the Pacific, millions of people who had no say in the decisions of European leaders were drawn into the fighting. This chapter looks at the truly global nature of the war, including the vast contributions of colonial troops, the forgotten battles fought far from the trenches of France, and the lasting impact the conflict had on the borders and politics of the wider world. It was a war that reshaped not just Europe, but the entire globe in ways that are still being felt today.

122. A Different Kind of War in Africa

Fighting in Africa looked nothing like the trench warfare of Europe. There were no endless belts of barbed wire or miles of zigzag trenches carved into the mud. In many places, there were no real "front lines" at all. Instead of sitting for months in fortified positions, soldiers were almost constantly on the move, marching across deserts, open savannas, and dense jungle where the map often showed little more than blank space. The war became less about holding ground and more about simply surviving the distance.

Campaigns stretched across enormous areas. Units might trek 200–300 miles (320–480 km) in a single month, sometimes covering more ground in one expedition than Western Front troops advanced in years. There were few roads and almost no railways, so columns hacked paths through brush with machetes, dragged artillery through mud, and hauled supplies over rocky ridges under a relentless sun. Boots rotted, uniforms tore, and rifles rusted from sweat and humidity long before an enemy was even sighted. Men grew exhausted not from battle, but from walking.

Even the landscape fought back. Rivers had to be crossed constantly for drinking water, washing, and moving supplies, yet many were murky, slow-moving channels teeming with wildlife. Crocodiles lurked just below the surface, perfectly camouflaged, sometimes snatching livestock (and occasionally men) who stepped too close to the banks. Soldiers wrote about porters vanishing midstream or being dragged under without warning, the water closing as if nothing had happened. Hippos, often mistaken for lazy and harmless, were in some ways even more dangerous. Highly territorial and weighing up to 3,000–4,000 pounds (1,400–1,800 kilograms), they could charge faster than a human could run, smash small boats, or overturn supply canoes with a single lunge. Nighttime crossings were especially tense, with splashes and grunts echoing through the dark. Beyond the rivers, the bush held its own hazards: venomous snakes hidden in tall grass, swarms of biting insects, and mosquitoes thick enough to darken the air at dusk. Animal attacks were rare compared to disease and exhaustion, but they added a constant edge of fear. In Africa, even something as simple as fetching water could feel like stepping into enemy territory.

When fighting finally came, it was rarely the massive, scheduled offensives seen in France. Instead, it felt like a chase. One force would appear briefly, fire a few shots, then vanish back into the bush, forcing the other side to pursue. Days or weeks might pass without contact, then suddenly erupt into a short, chaotic clash before the enemy slipped away again. Small patrols, ambushes, and skirmishes replaced the giant battles of the Western Front. Thick vegetation limited visibility to just a few yards, so soldiers often heard enemies moving before they saw them.

Mobility mattered more than fortifications. Speed, endurance, and knowledge of the terrain often decided survival. In Africa, the war wasn't about digging in and defending a trench. It was about who could keep marching the longest, who could navigate the wilderness, and who could outlast both the enemy and the environment itself.

123. The Enemy That Wasn't an Army

Disease proved deadlier than bullets for many forces operating in Africa. In some campaigns, sickness crippled armies long before they ever saw the enemy. Malaria, dysentery, sleeping sickness, typhoid, and heatstroke spread through camps with frightening speed, turning entire units weak and feverish within days. Mosquitoes rose in thick clouds at dusk, contaminating every bite with malaria parasites, while polluted rivers and stagnant water carried bacteria that caused violent stomach illnesses. A single drink could leave a soldier bedridden for weeks.

European troops, trained for cold European winters, were completely unprepared for tropical heat that regularly climbed above 100°F (38–40°C). Heavy wool uniforms trapped sweat, boots rotted in the humidity, and dehydration set in quickly during long marches. Men collapsed by the roadside with heat exhaustion, sometimes dying without ever firing a shot. Quinine, the main treatment for malaria, was often in short supply, and field hospitals were little more than tents with stretchers. Once sickness spread, there was often nowhere to evacuate the wounded.

The numbers were stark. In some African expeditions, more than half of a unit could be listed as "sick" at any given time, and for every man wounded in combat, several others were lost to disease.

124. The Carrier Corps and the Hidden Cost of War

Because railways and proper roads barely existed across much of Africa, armies could not rely on trains or trucks to move supplies. Instead, they depended on human muscle. Hundreds of thousands of local civilians were recruited or simply forced into service as porters. These men were not professional soldiers. Most were farmers, fishermen, laborers, and even teenage boys pulled from their villages with little warning. In British territory this system became known as the Carrier Corps.

Colonial officers often refused to arm large numbers of Africans, fearing rebellion and believing European troops should do the fighting. But the armies still needed food, ammunition, tents, rifles, and medical gear carried across hundreds of miles of bush and savanna. The solution was simple and brutal: use people instead of machines. In many areas, it took three to five porters just to keep one combat soldier supplied. A single battalion might require thousands of carriers trailing behind it like a moving supply line.

Each porter hauled loads weighing 45–65 pounds (20–30 kilograms), sometimes more, marching day after day through heat, mud, and disease with little rest and almost no medical care. Many went barefoot. Pay was low or nonexistent. Food was often worse than what the soldiers received.

The scale was enormous. In British East Africa alone, historians estimate that around one million porters were recruited during the war, compared to only a few hundred thousand fighting troops. And the death toll was staggering. Disease, exhaustion, and starvation killed an estimated 90,000 to 120,000 or more carriers, likely more than the number of soldiers lost in combat. Many deaths were never recorded at all. Entire villages lost their strongest workers, leaving fields untended and families without support.

125. Fighting Through the Bush of East Africa

The fighting itself was chaotic and intensely personal. In thick bush and jungle, visibility sometimes shrank to just a few yards. Tall grass swallowed entire patrols. Branches snapped underfoot. Gunfire could erupt suddenly from unseen positions, and soldiers often heard the enemy moving before they ever caught a glimpse of them. Battles were rarely grand formations clashing in open fields. They were short, sharp ambushes. A burst of rifle fire, a scramble for cover, then silence as one side melted back into the landscape.

No commander embodied this style of warfare more than German officer Paul von Lettow-Vorbeck. With a force that rarely exceeded 12,000–15,000 men (many of them African askari troops) he tied down Allied armies that sometimes numbered more than 100,000 across the region. Instead of defending territory, he focused on movement. Railways were sabotaged. Bridges were destroyed. Supply depots were raided. When pressed, he simply retreated deeper into remote terrain, forcing the Allies to chase him across thousands of miles over four years. His campaign stretched from German East Africa into modern-day Tanzania, Mozambique, and Zambia, continuing even after other fronts in Europe had collapsed.

For civilians, this kind of war was devastating. Villages might serve as temporary headquarters or supply depots one week and be abandoned or stripped bare the next. Armies seized grain stores, slaughtered livestock, and confiscated tools. Fields went untended as men were recruited or forced into service. In some regions, famine followed in the wake of marching columns. The war did not always arrive as artillery or gunfire. Sometimes it arrived as empty granaries and missing workers.

Communication across these vast territories was painfully slow. Messages traveled by runner, horse, or telegraph lines that could be cut or sabotaged. Units sometimes operated for days without clear instructions. When the Armistice was signed in Europe on November 11, 1918, news did not instantly ripple across Africa. Some forces continued moving and fighting for days before official confirmation reached them. Lettow-Vorbeck himself only agreed to cease hostilities after receiving verified news of Germany's surrender.

126. A Distant Country in a Global War

Even nations far from Europe were drawn into the conflict, sometimes for reasons that had little to do with the trenches themselves. In 1917, Siam (modern-day Thailand) declared war on Germany and Austria-Hungary, not because it was directly threatened, but as a calculated political move. Although never formally colonized, Siam had long been pressured by Western powers into "unequal treaties" that limited its trade, courts, and sovereignty. By joining the Allies, the king hoped to prove Siam was a modern nation worthy of equal treatment at the peace table. The country seized German ships and businesses at home and sent about 1,200–1,300 volunteers (including pilots, mechanics, and drivers) to Europe, where some trained with French forces and served on the Western Front. Their numbers were small compared to the great powers, but their presence was symbolic. Siamese troops even marched in the Paris Victory Parade in 1919, one of the few Asian nations represented. When the war ended, Siam successfully used its contribution to renegotiate those unequal treaties and reclaim greater independence, showing how even a limited role in a global war could reshape a country's future.

127. Where the ANZAC Story Began

For Australia and New Zealand, the First World War did not truly begin in the muddy trenches of France but on the rocky beaches of Gallipoli, thousands of miles from home. Before dawn on April 25, 1915, thousands of young soldiers from the newly formed Australian and New Zealand Army Corps, many of them teenagers who had never left their hometowns before boarding a ship, climbed down rope ladders into small boats and rowed toward the dark Turkish coastline. Navigation errors carried them to the wrong stretch of shore, where steep cliffs rose sharply above the water instead of the flat beaches planners had expected. As the first men stumbled onto the stones, Turkish defenders opened fire from the heights. Soldiers slipped on loose gravel, tangled in wire, and scrambled uphill under bullets, units mixing together in confusion as officers were killed within minutes. Many fought their first battle before even learning the names of the men beside them.

The campaign was meant to be a quick strike to knock the Ottoman Empire out of the war and open a supply route to Russia, but instead it dragged into eight months of stalemate that looked eerily like the Western Front. Both sides dug trenches only yards apart, trading sniper fire, grenades, flies, disease, and heat that spoiled food within hours. In summer, the smell of unburied bodies drifted across no man's land; in winter, freezing rain flooded dugouts and turned the ground to mud. By the end, more than 8,000 Australians were dead, a staggering loss for a country of fewer than five million people, meaning almost every town knew someone who never came home.

Ironically, the most successful part of the campaign came at the end. During the evacuation in late 1915, soldiers built clever self-firing rifles using dripping water tins to pull triggers automatically, left fires burning, and arranged supplies to make the trenches appear occupied. Under cover of darkness, tens of thousands slipped away silently to the beaches. When Turkish troops finally attacked, they found only empty trenches and cold tea mugs, the enemy gone without a sound.

Though Gallipoli was a military failure, it became something else entirely: a defining moment in national memory. Letters home spoke of "mateship," stubborn humor, and loyalty under impossible conditions, and the word "Anzac" slowly transformed from an acronym into a symbol of courage and endurance. More than a century later, Australians and New Zealanders still gather before sunrise each April 25 for Anzac Day services, standing quietly in the dark as bugles play the Last Post at the exact hour those first boats reached the shore. In a war fought on the other side of the world, Gallipoli remains deeply personal, a story of sacrifice that helped shape how two nations see themselves.

128. The Coin Game That Became an ANZAC Tradition

Australian soldiers carried their favorite gambling game with them wherever they went, and nowhere did it thrive more than the vast training camps of Egypt before Gallipoli. In 1914 and early 1915, tens of thousands of young "diggers" were stationed near Cairo and the pyramids, living for months in endless rows of canvas tents pitched in hot, windblown desert sand. Training filled the mornings, but afternoons and evenings brought long stretches of boredom, regular army pay, and little supervision. With nothing to spend money on except cheap food, beer, and cigarettes, gambling quickly became the main entertainment. Their game of choice was "two-up," played with two pennies and a small wooden paddle called a "kip." One man flipped the coins high into the air while a ring of soldiers crowded around shouting bets, calling "heads!" or "tails!" and waving notes and cigarettes. When the coins smacked down onto the wood, cheers or groans erupted instantly. Fortunes could change in seconds. Some men lost an entire week's wages in a single throw, while others walked away rich enough to buy drinks for half the camp.

The games grew loud and chaotic, with dust clouds, laughter, arguments, and coins clacking late into the night. Gambling was officially illegal, and military police occasionally stormed through the tents to break up what they called "two-up schools," scattering players in every direction. But officers often tolerated it because it kept morale high and burned off restless energy. The game followed Australians from Egypt to Gallipoli and later to the trenches of France, becoming as much a part of their identity as their slang and their reputation for irreverence. More than a century later, that tradition still survives: two-up remains illegal across Australia on every day of the year except one, Anzac Day, when coins are legally tossed in pubs and veterans' halls in memory of the soldiers who once played it between battles under the desert sun and distant pyramids.

129. The Hundred Days That Ended the War

For nearly four years the Western Front had barely moved. Men died by the hundreds of thousands for gains measured in yards. Verdun, the Somme, Passchendaele, each offensive followed the same pattern: weeks of artillery, then soldiers climbing out of trenches into machine guns, only to end up almost exactly where they started. It felt like the war might last forever. Then, in the late summer of 1918, something changed. Historians call it the Hundred Days Offensive, not a separate war but the final, relentless stretch of fighting that finally shattered Germany's ability to continue. It began on August 8, 1918, at the Battle of Amiens, and ended with the Armistice on November 11, roughly ninety-five to one hundred days later. In that short span, the most static war in modern history suddenly became fluid.

Instead of launching one giant, suicidal assault, the Allies changed tactics completely. Attacks were shorter, sharper, and better coordinated. Tanks rolled forward in waves to crush barbed wire. Aircraft spotted targets and strafed roads. Artillery fired creeping barrages that moved like a curtain of explosions just ahead of advancing troops. Infantry followed close behind rather than charging blindly. And most importantly, fresh American divisions were arriving by the tens of thousands, adding manpower the exhausted European armies no longer had. Rather than waiting months between battles, the Allies attacked again and again, hammering different points along the line so the Germans never had time to rest or rebuild.

Germany simply couldn't keep up. Years of blockade had left the country hungry. Supplies were short. Horses were dying. Ammunition stocks were thin. Reinforcements were scarce. Morale was cracking, and mutinies were already simmering. Against this, the Allies suddenly had new trucks, new shells, new food, and seemingly endless American replacements. The balance flipped almost overnight.

The shock came immediately. On the first day at Amiens, Allied forces advanced 10–12 kilometers, an almost unimaginable distance in a war where a few hundred meters had once cost thousands of lives. Tens of thousands of German soldiers surrendered in a single day. Entire units simply gave up rather than fight. German General Erich Ludendorff later called it "the black day of the German Army." From that moment on, Germany mostly retreated instead of attacking.

Over the next three months, the Allies smashed through the supposedly impregnable Hindenburg Line, retook huge areas of France and Belgium, and captured hundreds of thousands of prisoners. Railways collapsed. Supply lines failed. German soldiers marched backward faster than they had ever advanced. At home, food riots spread. Sailors mutinied. Workers struck. The government itself began to crumble. It became painfully clear that the war was no longer about victory but survival.

130. How the War Moved Power from London to New York

By the time American soldiers finally stepped into the trenches in 1918, the United States had already been fighting the war for years in a quieter but equally decisive way, with money. When the war began in 1914, London was the undisputed financial capital of the world. Britain controlled global trade routes, insured most of the world's shipping, lent money to other nations, and backed its powerful currency with vast gold reserves. The United States was wealthy but still secondary, an industrial giant that had not yet replaced Europe as the center of global finance. Four years later, that balance had completely flipped.

At first, Britain and France simply paid cash for American supplies. Then they paid in gold. Ship after ship crossed the Atlantic not with troops but with bullion, crates of gold bars hauled from European vaults and stacked into the holds of steamers bound for New York. The metal was used to buy American wheat, beef, coal, boots, rifles, trucks, and millions of artillery shells. By 1915 and 1916, so much gold had flowed west that Britain's reserves were nearly exhausted. The empire that had once financed half the planet was literally running out of metal. When the gold ran dry, they began borrowing.

The first lifeline came from Wall Street. In 1915, American bankers led by J.P. Morgan & Co. arranged what was then the largest foreign loan in history: a $500 million Anglo-French bond issue sold to American investors at 5 percent interest, repayable over about five years. It was only the beginning. As the war dragged on and costs exploded, the Allies kept ordering more supplies on credit. By early 1917, billions of dollars' worth of American goods were crossing the ocean every month, all paid for with borrowed money.

Then the United States entered the war in April 1917, and lending became official government policy. Washington began selling "Liberty Bonds" to its own citizens, encouraging ordinary Americans to invest their savings "to win the war." The money raised didn't stay at home. It was immediately lent to Britain and France. In effect, American families financed the Allied war effort directly. The sums were staggering. By the end of the conflict, the U.S. government had loaned the Allies roughly $10 billion in total. Britain alone owed about $4.6 billion to the United States government, on top of earlier private loans. France owed several billion more. At the time, those figures were almost unimaginable. In modern terms, Britain's debt alone would equal roughly $80–90+ billion today.

The terms were relatively soft but still heavy. Interest ran around 4 to 5 percent, sometimes deferred during the war itself. Afterward, formal agreements stretched payments over decades. Britain's 1923 settlement spread repayment across 62 years at reduced interest, requiring annual payments of around $160–170 million a year, the equivalent of billions annually today. In theory, Britain would still be paying into the late twentieth century. In practice, the strain was enormous. When the Great Depression hit in 1929, trade collapsed, unemployment soared, and government tax revenue shrank dramatically, making those yearly payments feel crushing. Britain struggled to meet installments, payments faltered or were temporarily suspended, and debts were repeatedly renegotiated. Then, before the old loans were even settled, the world slid into another catastrophe. World War II forced Britain to borrow vast sums from the United States all over again just to survive, layering fresh debts on top of the old ones. The result was a financial burden that stretched across generations. Astonishingly, Britain did not fully finish repaying its combined World War I and World War II debts to the United States until 2006, nearly ninety years after the first loans were taken out.

While Europe drained its gold and mortgaged its future, American industry boomed. Factories that once made consumer goods switched to rifles, trucks, engines, and shells. Steel mills poured out rails and artillery. Farms shipped mountains of grain and meat overseas. Shipyards launched freighters faster than German submarines could sink them. And because the American homeland was never bombed or invaded, none of this infrastructure was destroyed. While Europe's factories burned and fields became battlefields, American production only grew.

By 1918, the United States held close to half of the world's gold supply. The global financial center quietly shifted from London to New York. Before the war, nations borrowed from Britain. After the war, they borrowed from America. The change was permanent. Britain emerged victorious but financially crippled, weighed down by debt and reconstruction costs. The United States emerged richer, stronger, and suddenly the world's largest creditor. Power had crossed the Atlantic without a single shot being fired.

So when fresh American troops finally marched into France in 1918, they weren't just bringing rifles and uniforms. Behind them stood the full weight of a booming economy that could outproduce entire continents. In many ways, the war wasn't only won in the trenches. It was won in factories, banks, and shipyards thousands of miles away. And when the guns finally fell silent, the twentieth century no longer belonged to Europe. It belonged to America.

ELEVEN

The End & The Long Shadow

131. The Collapse of Germany

By the autumn of 1918, Germany was no longer losing the war in dramatic last stands or heroic defeats. It was simply coming apart. After four years of grinding conflict, the army that had once marched confidently across Europe now retreated day after day, step by step, across ground it had sworn never to surrender. Railways were shattered by artillery and air raids. Supply depots burned. Horses starved. Reinforcements barely existed. Units that had once numbered in the thousands sometimes mustered only a few hundred exhausted men. The illusion of stalemate that had defined the Western Front for years suddenly vanished, replaced by a steady, unstoppable backward drift.

The arrival of fresh American forces made the imbalance impossible to ignore. Every week brought new Allied divisions, new trucks, new tanks, new artillery. Germany, by contrast, had nothing left to replace its losses. Its soldiers knew the math. For every man they lost, the enemy seemed to gain two more. Rumors spread through the trenches about endless American arrivals, about factories across the Atlantic working day and night. The war no longer felt winnable. It felt infinite. Surrenders increased. Patrols hesitated. Entire groups gave up rather than die for ground that would be abandoned tomorrow anyway. German General Erich Ludendorff later called August 8, 1918, the opening of the Allied breakthrough at Amiens, "the black day of the German Army." From that moment on, retreat became routine.

But the collapse was not only military. It was psychological. After years of sacrifice, hunger, and grief, belief itself began to crumble. Orders still came down the chain of command, but they carried less and less weight. Officers could demand obedience, yet could no longer promise victory. Men who had survived Verdun and the Somme now asked a simple question: why keep fighting?

Behind the front lines, civilian Germany was unraveling just as quickly. The British naval blockade had strangled imports for years, leaving shelves empty and diets thin. By 1918, food shortages were severe. Bread was stretched with fillers. Meat was rare. Coal ran short in winter. Families queued for hours for basic rations that sometimes never arrived. Inflation eroded wages. Children grew malnourished. What had begun as patriotic endurance turned into quiet anger. Strikes spread through factories and shipyards, not as ideology at first, but as desperation. The home front that had once supported the war effort simply ran out of strength.

Then the breaking point came from below. In late 1918, sailors ordered to launch one final, suicidal attack against the British fleet refused. Mutinies erupted in the ports. Workers joined them. Protests spread from city to city with startling speed. Red flags appeared over town halls. Local councils replaced imperial officials. Authority dissolved almost overnight. It wasn't a carefully planned revolution. It was exhaustion made visible. After four years of total war, ordinary people simply stopped obeying.

Faced with an army that could no longer advance, a navy that would not sail, and civilians who would not sacrifice more, Germany's leaders confronted an unavoidable truth. Continuing the war would not save the nation, it would destroy it completely. There were no reserves left, no miracle weapons, no hidden strength waiting to be unleashed. The only option remaining was to ask for the fighting to stop.

So the request for an armistice went out, not as a bargaining move, but as an admission of reality. Germany had not been knocked down in a single blow. It had been worn out, militarily, economically, and emotionally. The empire that had entered the war confident and united now ended it hungry, fractured, and leaderless. Before the guns even fell silent, the old order had already collapsed. What remained was not defeat in one last battle, but the slow, unmistakable realization that the war had taken everything, and there was nothing left to give.

132. The Silence of the Armistice

When the end finally came, it did not look like victory parades or cheering crowds. It looked like paperwork, exhaustion, and surrender dressed up as negotiation. By November 1918, Germany had no real leverage left. Its armies were retreating, its navy mutinying, and its cities sliding into unrest. Continuing the war meant collapse or invasion. So German representatives were sent through the lines under a white flag to request an armistice, not to bargain as equals, but to accept whatever terms the Allies chose to impose.

The meeting took place far from any grand capital or ceremonial hall, deep inside the Forest of Compiègne in northern France. There, in a quiet railway clearing, stood a single railcar belonging to French Marshal Ferdinand Foch, the Supreme Allied Commander. The setting was deliberate. Isolated, controlled, and symbolic, it emphasized who held power and who did not. Inside the carriage, the German delegation was handed a list of demands and given little room to argue. The terms were not a compromise. They were instructions.

Germany was required to stop fighting immediately, withdraw from all occupied territories, and retreat behind the Rhine. Vast quantities of weapons had to be surrendered, including thousands of artillery guns, machine guns, aircraft, trucks, and railway engines. Much of the fleet was to be handed over. Allied prisoners of war were to be released at once, while German prisoners would remain in captivity. Perhaps most crushing of all, the Allied naval blockade would continue even after the shooting stopped, meaning food shortages at home would not immediately end. The message was clear. The war was over, but Germany would not dictate how.

The agreement was signed in the early hours of November 11, 1918. Yet the ceasefire was not set to begin immediately. It would take effect at 11 a.m., several hours later, to allow orders to reach armies stretched across hundreds of miles of front lines. The timing created a strange and tragic countdown. Fighting continued through the morning. Artillery still fired. Patrols still advanced. Men were still killed, some only minutes before the deadline, fully aware that the war was about to end. For them, peace came too late.

Then the moment arrived. The eleventh hour of the eleventh day of the eleventh month. After more than four years of constant gunfire, shell bursts, and engines, the noise simply stopped. No grand signal announced it. The cannons fell quiet one by one. Machine guns ceased. The air, which had trembled with explosions for years, settled into an unfamiliar stillness.

Many soldiers did not cheer. Some stood cautiously, unsure if it was real. Others sat down where they were, too tired to react. A few wept quietly. After living so long under the expectation of sudden death, silence itself felt unnatural. The landscape around them remained cratered and broken, littered with wire, mud, and graves. Nothing looked like victory. It looked like survival.

World War I did not end with celebration. It ended with relief, disbelief, and a quiet that felt heavier than the guns had ever sounded.

133. The Difficult Journey Home

When the guns fell silent, millions of soldiers faced a new and unexpected challenge: going home. Ending the war on paper was far simpler than dismantling armies that had grown to unprecedented size. Entire divisions needed to be processed, transported, documented, and discharged. Rail networks were damaged or overwhelmed. Camps overflowed with men waiting for orders that arrived slowly or not at all. Some soldiers waited weeks or even months before being officially released, stuck in a strange limbo between war and peace, unsure what came next.

For those who finally boarded trains and ships, the journey home carried a mix of anticipation and unease. Families imagined joyful reunions. Towns prepared celebrations. But the men returning were not the same ones who had left in 1914 or 1915. They stepped off trains thinner, older in the face, often quieter than expected. Many carried visible reminders of the war. Hundreds of thousands had lost limbs, eyesight, or mobility. Artificial legs and arms were fitted as best as technology allowed, but prosthetics were crude and uncomfortable. Veterans missing hands or legs had to relearn basic tasks in societies unprepared to provide long-term support. Governments struggled to supply pensions, rehabilitation, or meaningful employment for such vast numbers of disabled men.

Even for those without obvious wounds, reintegration proved difficult. Cities had changed. Jobs had disappeared or been filled. Prices had risen sharply. Inflation eroded savings. Industries that had boomed during wartime contracts slowed abruptly. Some returning soldiers found that the skills that had kept them alive in trenches and bombardments meant little in civilian life. The discipline of military structure vanished overnight, replaced by uncertainty.

Emotionally, the distance between veterans and civilians often felt just as large as the physical distance they had crossed. Families wanted stories of bravery and closure. Many soldiers had only confusion, grief, or silence to offer. Experiences of mud, bombardment, and constant death did not translate easily into conversation at a kitchen table. When they did speak, civilians often struggled to understand. When they stayed silent, misunderstandings grew. Shared experience created tight bonds among veterans, while separating them from those who had remained at home.

Years of following orders, watching friends die, and enduring promises of eventual victory had reshaped how many men viewed authority. Patriotic slogans sounded hollow after so much loss. Political speeches felt detached from reality. In defeated nations, resentment simmered. In victorious ones, triumph felt muted by the scale of sacrifice. Across Europe, returning soldiers carried not celebration, but skepticism.

The war had demanded everything from them. When they returned, they found that peace offered no simple reward. For millions, coming home was not a return to the world they remembered, but the beginning of a different struggle to understand what the war had taken and what, if anything, it had given back.

134. The Invisible Wounds of War

Not all wounds bled. As the war dragged on, armies began encountering a different kind of injury that confused and unsettled everyone who witnessed it. Soldiers who had survived months or years of combat sometimes broke down without warning. Strong, experienced men who had endured artillery barrages and machine gun fire suddenly trembled uncontrollably, stared into space, or collapsed in tears. Some lost the ability to speak. Others could not stop shaking. A few became frozen and unresponsive, unable to follow even the simplest orders. There were no visible cuts or broken bones, yet these men were as incapacitated as if they had been physically struck.

At first, doctors assumed the condition must be caused by exploding shells physically damaging the brain. The term "shell shock" reflected this early theory. But cases soon appeared in soldiers who had never been near a blast. It became clear that something else was happening. Weeks of sleepless nights, constant bombardment, the sight of friends killed without warning, and the unrelenting fear of sudden death pushed the human nervous system past its limits. The mind, like the body, could simply give out.

Military authorities struggled to understand what they were seeing. Some doctors argued that these men were suffering genuine psychological trauma and needed rest, safety, and time away from the front. Others saw the symptoms as weakness, cowardice, or even deliberate avoidance of duty. Because the injury left no visible scar, it was easy to doubt. In an army built on discipline and obedience, an invisible wound was often treated as a moral failure rather than a medical one.

The results could be cruel. Instead of compassion, some soldiers were punished or shamed. A few were threatened with court-martial. Others were subjected to harsh "treatments" meant to shock them back into reality, including electric currents, shouting, or forced drills. The message was clear. The body could be injured, but the mind was expected to endure indefinitely.

For those who survived and returned home, the symptoms rarely vanished with the armistice. Nightmares replayed bombardments long after the guns fell silent. Sudden noises triggered panic. Crowds felt overwhelming. Some veterans avoided sleep altogether. Others became withdrawn, irritable, or emotionally numb, unable to reconnect with families who remembered a different person. Loved ones often watched in confusion as husbands, sons, or brothers seemed changed in ways they could not explain.

Society had few answers. The language to describe psychological trauma barely existed, and long-term support was limited or nonexistent. Many veterans simply carried their suffering quietly for decades. Only years later would doctors begin to understand that what they had witnessed was not cowardice or weakness, but a natural response to prolonged terror. The modern term post-traumatic stress disorder would not be coined until much later, yet its reality had already shaped millions of lives.

World War I proved that industrial warfare could wound the mind as deeply and permanently as the body. Even when the fighting ended, for many survivors the war continued in memories they could not escape, battles replayed each night in the dark long after the world around them had finally found peace.

135. Remembering the Unknown

When the fighting stopped, the dead did not neatly return home with the living. Across Europe, the battlefields remained littered with the aftermath of four years of industrial killing. Shell craters, collapsed trenches, and shattered forests concealed bodies that had never been recovered. In earlier wars, most families could bury their loved ones in local cemeteries. In World War I, that simple ritual became impossible for millions. Entire units had vanished under artillery fire. Men were buried where they fell, often quickly and without ceremony, sometimes by comrades working under gunfire, sometimes by exhausted burial parties ordered to clear the ground before disease spread.

The scale of death overwhelmed any system meant to track it. Graves were dug hastily and marked with rough wooden crosses that rotted or were blown away. Shelling churned the earth so violently that burial sites were disturbed again and again, mixing remains together or erasing locations entirely. Artillery blasts shattered bodies and destroyed identification tags. Uniforms disintegrated in mud and rain. When teams later returned to exhume and rebury the fallen properly, they often found bones from several men intertwined with no reliable way to separate them. What earlier generations would have mourned as individual deaths increasingly became anonymous losses.

For families waiting at home, uncertainty could be worse than confirmation. Letters stopped. Names appeared on lists marked "missing" rather than "killed." Weeks stretched into months, then years, with no answers. Mothers, wives, and siblings lived with the quiet hope that perhaps their soldier had been captured or stranded somewhere far away. For many, that hope never fully faded because there was no body to prove otherwise. Grief without a grave felt unfinished.

In response, societies searched for new ways to mourn losses too vast to comprehend. Towns and villages began erecting memorials in public squares and churchyards, not to celebrate victory, but simply to record absence. Long columns of names were carved into stone, sometimes so many that they covered entire walls. In small communities, the lists could include nearly every young man of fighting age. These monuments became gathering places for collective remembrance, spaces where private sorrow turned into shared silence.

Out of this grief grew one of the most powerful symbols of the war: the Unknown Soldier. Since so many bodies could not be identified, one unidentified set of remains was chosen to represent them all. Buried with full military honors in national ceremonies, this single grave stood in for thousands who would never come home. In France and the United Kingdom, tombs of the Unknown Soldier became sacred spaces, guarded, visited, and covered in flowers year after year. The strength of the symbol lay in its anonymity. Without a name, the soldier could belong to anyone. Every family could imagine that their missing son rested there.

Remembrance itself changed. Earlier wars had favored statues of generals and triumph. After World War I, memorials were quieter, heavier, more somber. Ceremonies emphasized stillness rather than celebration. Moments of silence replaced cheers. The war had cost too much to glorify. It had taken too many lives to frame as victory alone.

By the early 1920s, the land still gave up reminders of the scale of loss. Farmers plowing former battlefields uncovered bones and fragments of uniforms. Construction crews unearthed forgotten graves. Even decades later, remains continued to surface, small proofs that the war had never been fully cleared away. For countless families, there would never be a marked resting place, only a name on stone and an empty chair at home.

In the end, World War I did not leave behind tidy cemeteries and closure. It left gaps. Gaps in families, gaps in towns, gaps in memory. The monuments and the Unknown Soldier did not solve that absence, but they gave it shape, allowing entire nations to mourn together for the millions who were lost without a trace.

136. The War That Still Lies Underground

Even after the dead were buried and the monuments raised, the war refused to fully leave the landscape. During four years of industrialized fighting, armies fired an estimated one billion artillery shells across Europe. Not all of them exploded. Millions failed to detonate on impact, burying themselves deep in churned soil or sinking into cratered fields. When the guns fell silent in November 1918, the ground itself remained armed.

In northern France and Belgium, entire regions were so saturated with unexploded munitions that authorities declared parts of the countryside permanently unsafe. Some areas became known as the "red zones," land considered too contaminated with explosives, chemicals, and human remains to safely farm or inhabit. Yet over time, as people returned to rebuild their lives, fields once scarred by trenches were plowed again. With each turn of the soil, metal rose to the surface.

Farmers began calling it the "iron harvest." Every year, plows struck artillery shells buried for decades. Rusted cylinders containing high explosives or poison gas emerged from the earth like relics from another age. Many remained dangerously unstable despite lying underground for a century. Bomb disposal teams in France and Belgium still collect hundreds of tons of World War I munitions annually. Some shells contain mustard gas or other chemical agents that have slowly corroded their casings, leaking toxins into surrounding soil and groundwater.

Accidents continue to happen. Construction workers uncover buried ordnance while laying foundations. Road crews disturb shells while repairing highways. Occasionally, civilians handling what appears to be harmless scrap metal trigger explosions that kill or injure more than a hundred years after the war officially ended. In some areas, children are warned never to touch strange metal objects found in fields because they might still be live.

The persistence of unexploded shells is a stark reminder of how intensely the land was bombarded. During major offensives, artillery fire was so heavy that the ground itself seemed to boil. Shells landed faster than they could be counted, turning fields into mud and forests into splintered stumps. Unlike monuments carved in stone, these remnants do not symbolize sacrifice or memory. They remain active threats, hidden beneath crops and grass.

More than a century later, World War I still demands caution from those who live where it was fought. The war may have ended in silence on November 11, 1918, but beneath the surface, fragments of it remain armed, waiting. The battlefield was never entirely cleared. It was simply buried.

137. When Empires Fell

When the shooting stopped, the damage was not limited to shattered towns and cratered fields. Entire political systems collapsed alongside the armies that had defended them. World War I did not simply defeat countries. It erased empires that had ruled for centuries. Governments that once appeared permanent vanished in a matter of months, leaving behind vast regions with no clear authority and no agreed future.

The German Empire fell first. As defeat became unavoidable, the Kaiser abdicated and fled into exile, ending a monarchy that had dominated central Europe. Soon after, the Austro-Hungarian Empire, a sprawling state that had stitched together dozens of languages and ethnic groups under one crown, splintered almost overnight. What had once been a single political unit fractured into separate national movements, each demanding independence. At the same time, the Russian Empire had already collapsed into revolution and civil war, while the Ottoman Empire, which had ruled much of the Middle East for hundreds of years, disintegrated under military defeat and occupation. By 1919, four great empires that had shaped Europe and its neighbors for generations were simply gone.

In their place, diplomats gathered around conference tables and began drawing new borders across maps that only partially reflected reality on the ground. Nations such as Poland, Czechoslovakia, and Yugoslavia were created or restored, carved from former imperial territory. On paper, these new states promised self-determination and freedom. In practice, the lines were often compromises sketched by negotiators far from the people who actually lived there. Rivers, railways, and strategic concerns mattered as much as culture or language.

As a result, millions of people woke up to find themselves foreigners in their own homes. Germans now lived inside Poland. Hungarians found themselves outside Hungary. Ethnic and religious minorities were scattered across borders that did not match where communities actually existed. Old rivalries that had once been contained within empires suddenly hardened into international disputes. What looked tidy on a map felt messy and unstable on the ground.

The same pattern unfolded beyond Europe. In the former Ottoman lands, Allied powers divided territory into "mandates" administered by Britain and France, claiming the regions were not yet ready for independence. Borders were drawn with straight lines across deserts and mountains, grouping together communities that had rarely shared governance while separating others that had long been connected. Decisions made in distant conference rooms reshaped the Middle East without consulting many of the people who lived there, planting tensions that would echo for generations.

The collapse of empire also changed how people thought about power itself. For decades, European empires had seemed invincible, their authority backed by vast armies and global wealth. The war shattered that illusion.

Soldiers and civilians alike had watched supposedly permanent systems crumble in just a few years. Monarchies fell. Flags changed. Capitals shifted. The old world order that had defined the nineteenth century disappeared faster than anyone thought possible.

Peace, it turned out, was not simply the absence of fighting. It was the beginning of a new, uncertain map. Instead of restoring stability, the end of the war created dozens of fragile states, disputed borders, and unresolved grievances. The guns had stopped, but the political shockwaves were only beginning, reshaping Europe, the Middle East, and much of the modern world in ways that would continue to unfold long after 1918.

138. The Lost Generation

When the war ended, the damage was not measured only in borders or ruined cities. It lived inside the people who had survived it. Across Europe, an entire generation carried the weight of four years spent in trenches, bombardments, and mass death. These were the young men who had marched off in 1914 believing they were heading toward adventure or glory. By 1918, many returned home older than their years, quieter, and deeply skeptical of everything they had once been told. Later writers would call them the "Lost Generation," not because they had disappeared, but because the world they had expected to inherit no longer existed.

Before the war, many Europeans trusted their governments, their monarchies, and the idea that progress was inevitable. After the war, those beliefs felt hollow. Millions had followed orders faithfully, watched friends die for yards of mud, and endured years of sacrifice, only to come home to unemployment, inflation, and political chaos. The promises of honor and victory rang empty against the reality of broken bodies and crowded cemeteries. For many veterans, it seemed that the people who had sent them to fight had never truly understood what the fighting cost.

This disillusionment shaped daily life. Former soldiers often struggled to settle into routines that once felt normal. Civilian problems seemed small compared to what they had endured, yet the lack of purpose felt equally unsettling. Factories, offices, and farms offered little of the structure or intensity they had grown used to. Some drifted from job to job. Others gathered mainly with fellow veterans who shared the same memories and frustrations. Among themselves, they could speak openly. With everyone else, there was often silence.

Politically, the consequences were profound. Faith in gradual reform weakened. Compromise felt pointless after years of total war. Many people no longer trusted traditional parties or cautious leaders. Instead, they gravitated toward movements that promised simple answers, strong leadership, and national revival. In defeated countries especially, humiliation and hardship mixed with anger. Veterans who felt their sacrifices had been wasted became receptive to anyone who claimed to restore pride and meaning.

In Germany and other unstable regions, former soldiers formed paramilitary groups that offered exactly what civilian life lacked. These organizations provided camaraderie, discipline, uniforms, and a clear sense of belonging. Marching together, drilling together, and following commands again felt familiar. Violence, which had once been confined to battlefields, began spilling into politics. Street fights, uprisings, and armed demonstrations became common as extremist groups battled for influence. The habits of war proved difficult to leave behind.

Even in victorious nations, the mood was darker than expected. Celebrations were muted by the sheer scale of loss. Nearly every town had lost sons, brothers, and fathers. Instead of triumph, many people felt exhaustion. Art, literature, and culture reflected this shift. Writers and poets described a world stripped of innocence. Optimism gave way to cynicism. The belief that modern society was steadily improving had been shattered by the most destructive conflict humanity had ever seen.

World War I had not simply redrawn maps. It had reshaped how millions of people thought about authority, sacrifice, and the future. The generation that came of age in the trenches returned home less trusting, less patient, and far more willing to embrace radical change. The war had taught them that entire systems could collapse in months and that violence could transform history overnight. Those lessons would echo through the decades that followed, influencing revolutions, uprisings, and the rise of new, more extreme political movements.

The fighting had ended, but the mindset it created did not. In many ways, the war's most lasting legacy was not the destruction it left behind, but the hardened attitudes of the people who survived it, a generation shaped by loss and searching for certainty in a world that no longer felt stable.

139. A World Transformed

When World War I ended, the world did not return to what it had been in 1914. Too much had broken. Too many systems had collapsed. The war did more than destroy armies and cities. It quietly rearranged the balance of power across the entire planet, reshaping politics, economies, and societies in ways that still define the modern world.

Before the war, Europe had stood at the unquestioned center of global power. London was the financial capital of the world. Empires controlled vast colonies across Africa, Asia, and the Middle East. European governments dictated trade, borders, and diplomacy. By 1918, that dominance had cracked. Britain and France had technically won, but they emerged exhausted, indebted, and physically scarred. Their industries were damaged, their populations depleted, and their economies strained by years of borrowing. Victory had left them weaker, not stronger.

Across the Atlantic, a different story unfolded. The United States, largely untouched at home by the fighting, had supplied food, weapons, money, and fresh troops on a scale no European nation could match. While Europe burned, American factories expanded. While European treasuries emptied, American banks filled. By the end of the war, the United States held enormous gold reserves and had become the world's largest creditor. Financial power shifted from London to New York, marking the beginning of a new era in which global influence increasingly flowed westward. Without conquering territory, America had become the strongest economic force on Earth.

The war also weakened the idea that empires were permanent. Millions of colonial soldiers from Africa, Asia, and the Caribbean had fought and died for European powers. They had seen those supposedly invincible empires struggle, retreat, and bleed like anyone else. When these men returned home, they carried new expectations. They had traveled, trained, and fought overseas. They had witnessed both European strength and European vulnerability. Many began to question why they should accept foreign rule at all. In the decades that followed, independence movements grew louder and more organized, fueled in part by veterans who knew that imperial authority was not untouchable.

Technologically, the war accelerated humanity into a new and more dangerous age. Airplanes, tanks, submarines, machine guns, poison gas, and industrial artillery had transformed battlefields into factories of destruction. Warfare was no longer limited by courage or cavalry charges. It became mechanical, efficient, and impersonal. Entire landscapes could be erased in hours. Civilians could be starved by blockades or bombed from the sky. The conflict showed that modern industry could produce death on a scale previously unimaginable, setting the blueprint for every major war that followed.

Even daily life changed. Governments had expanded their control over economies, transportation, and information to manage total war. Propaganda, rationing, mass production, and centralized planning became normal tools of the state. After the war, many of these powers did not fully disappear. The relationship between citizens and governments had shifted permanently toward larger, more interventionist systems.

Most of all, the war altered how people saw the future. The confident optimism of the late nineteenth century, the belief that science and progress would steadily improve life, faded in the face of mechanized slaughter and mass graves. Societies became more cautious, more fractured, and in some places more radical. Borders drawn in haste created tensions that would spark new conflicts. Disillusioned veterans reshaped politics. Fragile peace settlements planted the seeds of future wars.

By the time the world reached the 1920s, it was clear that World War I had not simply been another European conflict. It had been a turning point for humanity. Old empires had fallen. New nations had risen. Power had shifted across oceans. Entire generations had been marked by loss. The map looked different. The balance of wealth looked different. The way wars were fought looked different.

The guns fell silent in 1918, but the world they left behind was not the one that had existed before. In countless visible and invisible ways, the modern age began in the shadow of the First World War.

TWELVE

Unusual Moments

Every war has its strange, surprising, and hard-to-believe moments that don't fit neatly into any single category. World War I was no different. This chapter is a collection of the facts that stood out on their own, from bizarre coincidences and record-breaking feats to the lesser-known stories that fell through the cracks of the bigger narrative. These are the moments that make you pause and think, proving that even in the middle of the most devastating conflict in history, the world still found ways to be unpredictable.

140. Tricking the Snipers

Snipers ruled the trenches, and simply lifting your head above the parapet for a second could mean instant death. To fight back, soldiers began building fake targets to trick enemy marksmen into revealing themselves. Using papier-mâché, sandbags, straw, and old uniforms, they crafted realistic dummy heads and torsos, sometimes painting faces, adding helmets, or even placing cigarettes in the mouths to make them look alive. These "soldiers" were slowly raised on sticks or propped along the trench edge like men on watch. Enemy snipers, thinking they had spotted a careless target, fired immediately. The crack of the shot or puff of muzzle smoke gave away their hidden position, and friendly snipers could then shoot back within seconds. Some units staged entire scenes, fake bodies slumped over sandbags, helmets set just high enough to tempt a shot, even mock horses or supply figures made from sacks and wood. It became a strange form of deadly theater, where both sides tried to outsmart each other with props and illusions.

141. Those Who Refused to Fight

Not every man called to fight picked up a rifle. In Britain alone, around 16,000 men registered as conscientious objectors, refusing military service on religious, moral, or political grounds. Some were Quakers (members of a Christian pacifist group who believed killing was always wrong), while others rejected the war entirely. They quickly became targets of public anger. Strangers sometimes pinned white feathers, the symbol of cowardice, onto their coats in the street, and newspapers mocked them as "conchies" nicknamed 'conchies,' a shortened, often mocking slang for conscientious objectors. Many were arrested, court-martialed, and imprisoned for months or even years, treated more like deserters than civilians. A few were sent to harsh labor camps or forced into noncombat roles such as farming, road building, or stretcher bearing, risking their lives to save the wounded without carrying weapons themselves. Yet a large number still agreed to serve in noncombat roles, becoming stretcher-bearers, medics, or farm laborers. Unarmed, they followed assaults into shellfire to carry wounded men back from no man's land, sometimes making trip after trip across open ground while bullets snapped overhead. Refusing to kill did not mean avoiding danger; it often meant risking their lives to save others. In a society that celebrated sacrifice and heroism, their quiet refusal stood out sharply, reminding the nation that not everyone believed the war was worth fighting.

142. America's War at Home

In the United States, fear of the enemy reached beyond the battlefield and into everyday life. German-Americans, who had long been one of the country's largest immigrant groups, suddenly faced suspicion and hostility. Schools stopped teaching German, orchestras renamed "German" music, and even foods were rebranded, with sauerkraut becoming "liberty cabbage" and hamburgers called "liberty steaks." Towns changed German street names, and some families avoided speaking their native language in public. A war fought across the ocean quietly reshaped culture at home, erasing traces of German identity almost overnight.

143. The Flower That Became a Symbol

One of the most enduring symbols of the war grew from a single moment of grief on the battlefield. In May 1915, after a brutal artillery bombardment near Ypres, Canadian army doctor John McCrae helped bury a close friend killed by a shell. The next morning, he noticed something strange and beautiful: bright red poppies blooming across the torn earth between fresh graves. The seeds had been stirred up by the digging and the explosions, turning the battlefield into a field of flowers. Sitting on the back of an ambulance, McCrae scribbled a poem beginning with the now-famous line, *"In Flanders fields the poppies blow, between the crosses, row on row."*

At first, he disliked the poem and reportedly tossed it away, but another officer rescued it and sent it to a magazine, where it spread rapidly through newspapers across the Allied world. Soldiers memorized it, families clipped it out, and the poppy quickly became a symbol of both sacrifice and remembrance. After the war, a teacher named Moina Michael began wearing a small red poppy in honor of the dead and started selling handmade versions to raise money for veterans. The idea spread internationally, and millions of paper poppies are still sold each year around November 11, with the money supporting former soldiers and their families.

144. Saving Lives Under Fire

Under the laws of war, doctors, nurses, and stretcher-bearers were not supposed to be targets at all. International agreements like the Geneva Conventions classified medical personnel as noncombatants, meaning they carried no weapons and were protected from deliberate attack. To mark their status, they wore white armbands with red crosses and worked under tents, wagons, and hospital roofs painted with the same symbol, a clear signal to enemy troops: do not fire. In theory, anyone treating the wounded was off-limits. In practice, the battlefield rarely respected theory. Artillery shells did not distinguish between soldiers and medics, air raids missed their marks, and stretcher-bearers often had to walk upright across open ground carrying heavy loads, making them easy targets. Casualty rates among medical teams could be shockingly high. The red cross offered legal protection, but not safety, and many of the men who came to save lives ended up losing their own.

145. The Villages That Never Returned

Entire towns simply disappeared because of the war. Across northern France and Belgium, villages that had existed for centuries were reduced to rubble so completely that they were never rebuilt. Constant shelling flattened houses, churches, schools, and roads until nothing remained but broken brick, twisted metal, and poisoned soil. Forests were shredded into splinters, wells filled with debris, and farmland churned so deeply by craters that it resembled the surface of the moon. In some places the destruction was so severe that governments declared the land permanently uninhabitable, marking it as part of the "Red Zone," where unexploded shells, chemicals, and buried bodies made rebuilding too dangerous. A few of these communities still exist only on maps and memorial signs, officially listed as villages that "died for France," with no residents but still recognized as towns out of respect for what was lost.

146. When the Battlefield Refuses to Disappear

In parts of France and Belgium, the First World War is still not entirely over. More than a century after the last shots were fired, farmers, construction crews, and road workers continue to dig up live artillery shells, grenades, and buried munitions left behind in the soil. During the war, millions of shells failed to explode on impact, sinking harmlessly into mud only to remain armed underground. Each year, an estimated hundreds of tons of unexploded ordnance are still recovered in what locals call the "iron harvest," as plows regularly strike rusted bombs the way earlier generations struck stones. Specialized bomb disposal teams travel from village to village collecting piles of old shells stacked at field edges like firewood before safely detonating them. Some still contain deadly gas or unstable explosives and can kill instantly if disturbed. Farmers are taught to leave anything metal untouched and call authorities instead. Entire areas of the former front, especially inside the old Red Zone, remain too dangerous to live on or farm properly.

147. Letters That Arrived a Century Late

Not everything left behind by the war was deadly. Sometimes, what the earth gives back is heartbreakingly human. Across former battlefields in France and Belgium, construction crews and farmers occasionally uncover bundles of old mail bags, sealed tins, or rusted boxes filled with letters that were never delivered. Some were dropped when trenches collapsed, others lost during retreats, or buried when shells destroyed field post offices. Decades later, mud preserves the paper surprisingly well. Inside are ordinary words frozen in time: sons telling mothers they're safe, husbands promising they'll be home by Christmas, soldiers describing muddy boots, bad food, or the hope that the war will end soon. Many of the writers were killed days or even hours after putting pen to paper, never knowing their final messages never arrived.

In some cases, archivists or volunteers still try to track down surviving relatives and deliver the letters a century late. For families, opening one can feel like hearing a voice from the past speaking directly across generations.

148. The Ghosts of Mons

After the Battle of Mons in August 1914, as exhausted British troops retreated under heavy German pressure, rumors began spreading of something impossible on the battlefield. Soldiers claimed that shadowy figures had appeared between the lines during the fighting, protecting them from enemy fire. Some described glowing shapes or silent men standing in the smoke. Others swore they saw medieval archers, like ghosts from England's past, firing invisible arrows into the advancing Germans. A few simply said "angels" had shielded them. The stories spread rapidly through the ranks and then back home through letters and newspapers, where they were repeated as miracles. Churches printed pamphlets celebrating divine protection for British troops.

The truth turned out to be stranger in a different way. Around the same time, a popular short story had been published in London describing phantom archers from the Battle of Agincourt returning to defend modern soldiers. Readers mistook the fictional tale for a real report, and as frightened, sleep-deprived troops shared rumors in muddy trenches, imagination and memory blurred together. Historians later concluded that most sightings were likely tricks of light, smoke, and exhaustion, or simply stories that grew in the telling. Yet the legend stuck.

149. Living Beneath the Battlefield

For long stretches of the war, many soldiers barely lived above ground at all. In heavily shelled sectors of the Western Front, the surface became so dangerous that entire units moved underground, digging deep into hillsides and trench walls like human moles. What began as simple holes for shelter slowly expanded into sprawling tunnel systems with timber supports, staircases, bunks, kitchens, aid posts, and even small chapels. Some dugouts sank 20 to 40 feet (6–12 meters) below the surface, deep enough to survive most artillery. From above, the battlefield looked empty, but beneath the mud thousands of men were sleeping, eating, and waiting in the dark.

Life underground was safer from shells but miserable in other ways. The air was damp and stale, heavy with smoke, sweat, and the smell of wet earth. Candles and oil lamps barely pushed back the darkness. Water seeped constantly through the walls, turning floors slick with mud. Rats and lice thrived. The ceilings were often so low that men couldn't stand upright, forcing them to crouch or crawl between rooms. When artillery landed nearby, the whole structure shook and rained dirt from the roof, making soldiers fear collapse or burial alive. Some described the sensation as living inside a coffin that might cave in at any moment.

Days blurred together without sunlight. Men slept in shifts on rough wooden bunks or directly on the ground, emerging only for sentry duty or patrols before disappearing back below. In places like Vimy Ridge and Messines, the underground networks grew so extensive that they resembled small buried towns, complete with signs, storage rooms, and hundreds of feet of corridors. To many soldiers, trench warfare no longer felt like fighting on land at all, but like existing beneath it, as if the war had forced humanity underground.

150. When Forests Turned to Matchwood

In some parts of the Western Front, entire forests simply ceased to exist. Years of constant artillery fire shredded trees so completely that what had once been green woods became fields of splintered stumps and broken poles. Shell after shell tore through trunks, snapping them like matchsticks and blasting branches into flying shards. Leaves vanished. Bark was stripped away. What remained looked less like nature and more like a giant pile of kindling scattered across the mud. Soldiers began calling these areas "matchwood forests," because every tree had been smashed into thin, jagged sticks.

From a distance, the landscape looked almost lunar. No shade, no birdsong, no grass, just gray mud and blackened timber stretching to the horizon. In places like the Somme, Verdun, and Passchendaele, woods that had stood for centuries disappeared in a matter of weeks. Landmarks vanished so completely that maps became useless. Units got lost crossing open ground where forests were supposed to be. Rain filled shell craters with stagnant water, and broken roots poked up like bones from the earth. The smell of churned soil mixed with smoke and decay.

Even after the war ended, the damage lingered. Many forests had to be replanted from scratch, and some areas were so polluted with metal fragments, chemicals, and unexploded shells that trees struggled to grow back for decades. Photographs from the time show soldiers walking through what look like graveyards of trees, thin wooden spikes stretching skyward in every direction.

151. When It Was Simply "The Great War"

When the fighting began in 1914, nobody called it "World War I." The name didn't exist yet, because no one imagined there would ever be a second one. At first, most people believed the conflict would last only a few months. Newspapers spoke confidently of "the war" or "the present war," assuming it would be short and decisive. In Britain it was often called simply "The Great War," meaning the biggest war anyone had ever seen, not the first of many. Others used phrases like "The European War," since most of the early fighting centered on France, Belgium, Germany, and Russia. Germans called it der Weltkrieg ("the world war") surprisingly early on, recognizing how many empires were involved, while Americans, before joining, often referred to it as "the European conflict."

As the months dragged into years and colonies from Africa, India, Australia, Canada, the Middle East, and Asia were pulled in, the scale became undeniable. Soldiers joked grimly that it was "the war to end all wars," a hopeful phrase repeated by politicians and newspapers who believed the suffering would be so terrible that humanity would never allow another one. That optimism aged badly. Only after a second global catastrophe erupted in 1939 did historians need a new label. The earlier conflict was retroactively renamed "World War I," or "the First World War," a title that quietly admitted the unthinkable: the "war to end all wars" had only been the beginning.

152. The War's Forgotten Horses

In an army that could replace men with new conscripts but struggled to replace animals, horses were often treated as more valuable than the soldiers riding beside them. World War I still depended heavily on horsepower. Before tanks and trucks fully took over, nearly everything moved by animal: artillery guns, ammunition wagons, food carts, ambulances, and supply trains. A single heavy gun might require six to eight horses just to drag it through mud. If the horses died, the gun stayed where it was, no matter how urgent the battle.

Because of that, horses were expensive, scarce, and strategically critical. A trained artillery horse could cost the equivalent of several months or even years of a soldier's pay. They had to be bred, raised for years, trained to ignore gunfire, and shipped across oceans. Replacing one wasn't quick.

Replacing a human soldier, harshly, often meant issuing another rifle to the next recruit.

This led to uncomfortable priorities. Veterinary units were sometimes better supplied than frontline medics. There are documented cases where wounded horses were evacuated by wagon while lightly wounded soldiers were told to walk. Armies kept detailed veterinary hospitals, dental care for horses, and special rations of oats and hay even when men lived on hard biscuits and weak tea. Commanders understood the math: save the horse, and you could still move food, shells, or the wounded. Lose the horse, and entire units might starve or be stranded.

The scale was enormous. All sides together used roughly 8–10 million horses and mules during the war, and millions died from shellfire, exhaustion, disease, or starvation. Soldiers often grew deeply attached to them, grooming and feeding the same animals every day. Many diaries mention grieving more openly for a dead horse than for another man, partly because the animal had been a constant companion, partly because it felt so unfair that something so loyal had no choice in the war at all.

153. Ancient Beasts in a Modern War

In the Middle East, British, Australian, New Zealand, and Indian forces relied heavily on camels. Thousands were organized into full camel corps, especially in Sinai and Palestine, where wheeled vehicles simply sank into soft sand. A single camel could carry 300–400 pounds (135–180 kilograms) of supplies and travel long distances without water, making it perfect for desert patrols and raids. Soldiers rode them for days across empty landscapes, rifles and machine guns strapped to their saddles, sometimes dismounting to fight on foot before climbing back on and vanishing into the dunes. The Imperial Camel Corps became so common that entire battles featured lines of camels instead of horses, an image that looked centuries old despite the presence of modern rifles and artillery.

Elsewhere, even stranger sights appeared. In parts of India and Southeast Asia, elephants were used to haul heavy artillery pieces, timber, and ammunition through jungle terrain where wheels couldn't pass. Their strength allowed them to drag guns up muddy slopes or across rivers that would have stopped tractors cold. Photographs show elephants harnessed to cannons or supply sleds, moving war material through thick forests like living cranes. Oxen and buffalo pulled carts in Africa. Donkeys and mules carried loads in mountain regions where nothing else could climb.

To soldiers arriving from the Western Front, it felt surreal. One month they might be slogging through Belgian mud behind barbed wire. The next, they were riding camels past palm trees, escorting caravans, or watching elephants drag artillery through the brush. The same war that produced tanks, machine guns, and poison gas also relied on animals that hadn't changed since ancient empires.

154. Battles for the Bridges

In a war that often looked like endless trenches and open fields, some of the most important battles were fought not for hills or towns, but for simple pieces of infrastructure: bridges. Rivers were natural barriers that could stop entire armies cold. Artillery, supply wagons, ambulances, and thousands of marching men could not simply wade across deep water. Without a bridge or a crossing point, an advance stalled instantly. So a single narrow span of wood or steel could become more valuable than a whole city.

Commanders planned offensives around these choke points. If you captured a bridge intact, your army could pour across in hours. If the enemy blew it up, repairs might take days or weeks under fire. That delay could mean running out of ammunition, food, or reinforcements. In fast-moving moments of the war, especially in 1914 and again in 1918, the difference between victory and failure sometimes came down to whether engineers could throw a temporary bridge across a river before nightfall.

Because of this, bridges were prime targets. Retreating armies often wired them with explosives and destroyed them at the last possible second. Engineers carried demolition charges specifically for this job. Meanwhile, advancing troops raced to seize crossings before they were blown, sometimes charging straight at the structure under machine-gun fire. Entire units were sacrificed just to hold one bridge long enough for the rest of the army to cross.

When bridges were gone, soldiers improvised. Combat engineers built "pontoon bridges" from floating metal or wooden sections lashed together, sometimes overnight. Others used ferries, barges, or planks laid over barrels. These makeshift crossings were shaky, crowded, and terrifying under shellfire. A single artillery hit could dump dozens of men and horses into the water. Still, they kept coming, because without that link, nothing behind the line could move forward.

Railway bridges were even more critical. One destroyed rail crossing could cut off thousands of tons of shells and food per day. Whole offensives slowed or collapsed simply because trains couldn't pass. Maps often marked bridges with heavy red circles, like arteries in a body. Block one, and everything downstream weakened.

155. Walls Made of Mud

For all the machine guns, artillery, and poison gas, one of the most important pieces of equipment on the Western Front wasn't a weapon at all. It was a simple burlap sack filled with earth. Sandbags shaped the entire battlefield. Without them, trenches would have collapsed, flooded, or offered almost no protection. With them, armies built miles of walls strong enough to stop bullets and even absorb shell fragments.

Every trench you see in photos, the neat parapets, the raised firing steps, the curved corners, was held together by thousands upon thousands of these bags. Soldiers filled them by hand using small shovels, tying them off and stacking them like bricks. A single firing bay might require hundreds. A whole trench sector might need tens of thousands. Across the Western Front, millions were used at any given time.

They worked because dirt stops bullets surprisingly well. A tightly packed sandbag could catch rifle rounds and shrapnel that would tear straight through wood or thin metal. Several layers thick could even blunt the blast of nearby shells. When artillery hit, the bags burst open and spilled dirt rather than exploding into deadly fragments like stone or concrete would. In a strange way, mud was safer than brick.

But sandbags were also endless labor. Rain rotted the fabric. Rats chewed holes through them. Shellfire shredded walls in seconds. After every bombardment, soldiers spent hours repairing damage, refilling sacks, rebuilding parapets, and stacking them again. It was common to work all night simply replacing what had been destroyed that afternoon. Trench life often meant digging and filling bags more than actually fighting.

They had other uses too. Men built dugout roofs from them, lined sleeping areas for insulation, propped them under stretchers as pillows, or used them as makeshift seats. Some were stuffed into coats as extra protection. Others became emergency barricades when raids broke through. If a section collapsed, the first order was always the same: "Get sandbags up."

Ironically, the war consumed so many that shortages became serious. Civilians at home were asked to donate old sacks. Farmers and factories shipped millions overseas. Entire supply trains carried nothing but empty bags. The front was constantly hungry for more.

156. The Trench Watch Revolution

Before World War I, most men didn't wear watches on their wrists at all. Timepieces were carried in waistcoat pockets on chains, and wristwatches were widely seen as delicate jewelry for women. But trench warfare made pocket watches almost useless. Reaching into your coat while climbing a ladder, fixing bayonets, or waiting for an artillery barrage could be slow, clumsy, or even fatal. Attacks were timed to the minute. Barrages lifted at exact seconds. "Stand-to" happened before dawn on the dot. In modern industrial war, seconds mattered, and soldiers needed both hands free.

So men improvised. They began strapping small pocket watches to their wrists with leather bands or sewing loops onto sleeves. Manufacturers quickly noticed and started producing purpose-built "trench watches" with tougher cases, thicker glass, luminous numbers, and sometimes metal cage grills over the face to stop shrapnel cracks. Dials were painted with glowing radium so time could be read in pitch darkness inside dugouts or during night attacks. For the first time, timekeeping became a piece of battlefield equipment, as essential as a rifle or compass.

The war quietly created an entire new industry. Swiss and American makers like Omega, Longines, Waltham, Elgin, and Zenith supplied thousands of rugged military watches, and many of those brands built their reputations on reliability under fire (companies like Casio wouldn't appear until decades later, but the idea of the tough, utilitarian wristwatch traces directly back to these trench models). When millions of soldiers returned home already used to wearing watches on their wrists, the fashion never went away. The modern men's wristwatch was essentially born in the trenches.

But there was a hidden cost. The glowing paint that made night reading possible contained radium, a radioactive substance. Factory workers, often young women, painted tiny numbers by hand and were told to shape their brushes with their lips for fine tips, unknowingly swallowing radium dust every day. Years later many suffered horrific jaw decay, anemia, bone fractures, and cancers in what became some of the first major industrial radiation poisoning cases. What began as a small wartime convenience (being able to check the time in the dark) helped expose the dangers of radiation and changed workplace safety laws forever.

157. From Shrapnel to Souvenirs

After heavy shelling, the battlefield floor changed completely. Explosions churned the earth like a plow, flipping mud, sandbags, and buried debris to the surface. When the smoke cleared, the ground glittered with fragments of war: jagged pieces of shrapnel, twisted shell casings, flattened bullets, and shards of steel torn from artillery rounds. Soldiers learned to spot them instantly. They called the fragments "trench teeth," because the sharp bits of metal stuck out of the dirt like broken fangs.

During quieter hours, men casually scavenged the ground, pockets filling with scraps that had screamed through the air only hours earlier. It became a strange ritual. After surviving a bombardment, some would walk the cratered earth almost like beachcombers, picking through the wreckage for interesting shapes or large fragments. A curved piece of brass might become a ring. A shell driving band could be hammered flat into a bracelet. Spent bullets were carved into crosses, pendants, or tiny sculptures. Larger shell casings were engraved with names, dates, or the word "France" and turned into vases or cups.

Entire dugouts sometimes doubled as miniature workshops. Using penknives, files, or bits of sandpaper, soldiers polished metal until it shone gold or copper. Others etched unit badges, hometowns, or sweethearts' initials into the surface. Some mailed these pieces home as gifts; others kept them in their packs as lucky charms or proof that they had survived another day.

158. Between the Trenches and Home

British soldiers had a slang word for home: "Blighty," a term borrowed from Hindi *bilāyat*, meaning Britain or the homeland. In the trenches, it took on an almost magical meaning. Blighty wasn't just a place. It meant warmth, clean sheets, real food, and safety far from artillery. So when men spoke of a "Blighty wound," they didn't mean just any injury. They meant one perfectly balanced between danger and relief: serious enough to be evacuated back to England, but not so severe that it killed or permanently crippled them.

A bullet through the arm. Shrapnel in the calf. A fractured hand.

Something painful but survivable. Something that meant a hospital bed and a ship home instead of another winter in the mud.

It created a strange, uncomfortable psychology. After months in the front line, with lice, shellfire, and friends dying daily, some soldiers quietly admitted they wouldn't mind a "nice little Blighty." Rumors circulated of men exposing a hand above the parapet a second too long, or standing a bit too high during an advance, hoping for a grazing wound. A few even shot themselves in the foot, though this was rare and harshly punished if discovered, sometimes treated as self-inflicted injury or desertion.

If a soldier was suspected of deliberately wounding himself to escape the front, the army treated it not as fear or exhaustion but as a crime. These injuries were officially labeled "self-inflicted wounds" or "self-mutilation," and officers took them very seriously. Military doctors examined the damage closely, looking for signs that the shot had come from close range, such as powder burns, torn fabric, or the angle of entry. A bullet through the hand or foot fired from only a few inches away was suspicious. Witnesses were questioned, rifles inspected, and if the story didn't add up, the man could be arrested and charged.

Punishments were harsh and meant to discourage others. Minor cases might mean loss of pay, extra drills, confinement, or being sent straight back to the trenches once healed. More serious cases went to court-martial and could lead to months in prison, demotion, or "Field Punishment No. 1," where a soldier was strapped upright to a post or wheel for hours a day in public view, exposed to the weather as a warning to everyone else. In the early years of the war, some armies even imposed the death penalty for desertion or deliberate injury. Britain alone executed more than 300 soldiers for offenses including cowardice and self-inflicted wounds. Most never acted on the thought, but the fact that the idea existed at all spoke volumes.

159. Eating the Enemy's Rations

Trenches rarely stayed neatly "British" or "French." Along much of the Western Front the Allied armies were mixed together, with neighboring sectors sometimes only a few hundred yards apart. British, Canadian, Australian, and French units regularly rotated through one another's lines, borrowed dugouts, shared roads, or took over recently captured enemy trenches. After an attack, soldiers might suddenly find themselves living in a German or French position for days or weeks, using whatever supplies had been left behind. That meant eating whatever food was available too.

Raids and advances often ended with an unexpected prize: enemy rations. German black bread, sausages, tinned meats, and pickles were eagerly collected, while French trenches were famous for their bread, cheese, and especially wine. French troops were officially issued wine as part of their daily ration, sometimes half a liter (about a pint) or more, something British soldiers almost never received. To men used to hard biscuits, bully beef, and endless tea, these captured supplies felt like luxury. Letters home frequently joked that "the Boche eat better than we do" or that French bread tasted like a feast.

160. The Frozen Trenches

Cold weather on the Western Front wasn't just uncomfortable, it was its own kind of enemy. For nearly four to five months each year, roughly November through March, temperatures hovered near freezing or below it almost constantly. In northern France and Belgium, winter days often sat around 30–40°F (0–5°C), while nights regularly dropped below 25°F (−4°C), and during cold snaps could fall near 10–15°F (−9°C to −12°C). Snow didn't cover the ground all winter, but there were often dozens of snow or sleet days each season, mixed with freezing rain that soaked uniforms by day and turned them stiff with ice by night. Worse than the snow was the endless cycle of thaw and freeze: trenches filled with water during the day, then hardened into icy sludge after sunset.

Men slept in damp greatcoats with boots still on because removing them meant frozen leather in the morning. Rifles iced up. Fingers went numb so quickly that loading ammunition or pulling a trigger became clumsy and painful. Water bottles froze solid. Tea turned lukewarm within minutes. Frostbite and trench foot multiplied as wet socks never fully dried. Sentries stamped their feet for hours just to keep blood moving, and some woke to find the duckboards glazed with ice like a skating rink.

161. From Private to President

From the moment a civilian's name was called in the draft to the moment a president or king made a decision, the war followed a rigid chain of command that stretched from muddy trenches to marble government halls. A conscript began at the very bottom as a private, the lowest rank and the backbone of every army, carrying a rifle, digging trenches, and following orders without question. Ten or twelve privates formed a section or squad led by a corporal. Several squads made a platoon commanded by a lieutenant. Four platoons formed a company under a captain. Several companies became a battalion led by a major or lieutenant colonel. Multiple battalions formed a regiment or brigade under a colonel or brigadier. Brigades grouped into divisions commanded by major generals, divisions into corps led by lieutenant generals, and several corps into entire field armies under full generals. Above them sat theater commanders planning entire fronts, then the national high command or general staff coordinating strategy for the whole war. At the very top were civilian leaders, presidents, prime ministers, or monarchs, who technically held ultimate authority and decided when to attack, negotiate, or continue fighting. In theory, orders flowed cleanly down this pyramid from the head of state to the newest private. In practice, a decision made in a quiet office hundreds of miles away could take days to reach the front, finally arriving as a shouted command from a mud-stained sergeant telling exhausted men to climb a ladder and go "over the top." For most soldiers, the vast hierarchy above them felt invisible. They rarely saw anything higher than their company officer, yet their lives were shaped by choices made by people they would never meet.

162. When Friends Went to War Together

One recruiting idea that seemed comforting at first ended up making the war's losses far more devastating at home. Early in the conflict, Britain raised what were called "Pals battalions," encouraging friends, brothers, factory workers, and even entire football teams or neighborhoods to enlist together. Posters promised that men could serve "shoulder to shoulder with your mates," and thousands signed up believing it would feel less frightening if everyone they knew went with them. Training camps often looked like hometown reunions, with clerks, miners, shopkeepers, and students sleeping in the same tents and joking that they'd bring their local rivalries to the front.

But when these battalions finally went into battle, they fought together and died together. On the first day of the Somme in 1916, some Pals units were nearly wiped out within hours. In places like Accrington, Barnsley, Leeds, and Sheffield, hundreds of men from the same streets fell in a single morning. Back home, the losses didn't trickle in one by one, they arrived all at once. Telegram boys walked door to door down entire blocks, knocking again and again. Schools lost former students by the dozens. Factories lost whole shifts of workers. Football clubs lost entire squads. In some towns, almost every family knew someone who would never return.

What had begun as a clever recruiting tactic turned into a shared tragedy. Instead of grief spread over months or years, whole communities were struck in a single blow, leaving empty classrooms, silent workshops, and gaps in family trees that never fully healed.

163. The Trains That Started the War

Mobilization in 1914 was so massive and mechanical that it was almost impossible to hide, and once it began, other nations could see it happening in real time. Railways were the backbone of every army's war plan, and moving millions of men required thousands of trains running on precise schedules. The moment mobilization orders were issued, ordinary life changed overnight. Civilian trains were canceled or delayed as tracks were handed over to the military. Railway stations filled with reservists hugging families goodbye, clerks pinning orders to notice boards, and long lines of soldiers climbing into crowded carriages with rifles and packs. Steam engines hissed and belched smoke day and night as troop trains rolled east or west without stopping. From a distance, it looked less like preparation and more like an exodus.

There was nothing secret about it. Horses, artillery pieces, wagons, and supply carts clogged roads near the borders. Telegraph wires buzzed constantly with coded military messages. Diplomats, journalists, and spies stationed in foreign cities simply had to step outside to see the evidence. Embassy staff reported that platforms were jammed with uniforms and that trains left every few minutes loaded with troops. Intelligence officers counted railcars through binoculars. In some countries, mobilization notices were even printed openly in newspapers or nailed to town halls, summoning every able-bodied man to report immediately. Church bells rang. Postmen delivered orders. Entire towns seemed to empty overnight.

The problem was that mobilization looked exactly like an invasion. There was no such thing as a slow or "defensive" buildup. War plans depended on strict timetables: trains had to run in a precise order, each one delivering a specific unit to a specific place at a specific hour. If the sequence stopped, the entire system collapsed into chaos. So once a country started loading trains, it was nearly impossible to pause or reverse. Leaders feared that waiting even a day could mean the enemy reached the border first with hundreds of thousands of men already in position.

As a result, mobilization triggered panic. If Russia began moving troops, Germany felt compelled to mobilize immediately. If Germany moved, France followed. Each government watched the others through reports and rumors, convinced that delay meant disaster. Diplomats were still arguing for peace while, at the same time, millions of soldiers were already rolling toward the front in packed railcars. In this way, the railways turned Europe into a giant machine. Once the first gears started turning, the rest were forced to move with them, and stopping the war became almost impossible before it had even officially begun.

164. The Night the Taxi Fleet Became an Army

When the German army surged toward Paris in September 1914, the French government suddenly faced a desperate problem: there weren't enough trains or trucks to move reinforcements fast enough to stop them. Rather than wait, officials turned to something completely ordinary, the city's taxi fleet. Almost overnight, hundreds of bright red Parisian taxicabs were commandeered, their meters still attached, their drivers still in caps and jackets, and ordered to the front.

On the night of September 6–7, around 600 taxis lined up beneath streetlamps and drove through the dark in long convoys, carrying thousands of soldiers toward the Battle of the Marne. Each car squeezed in five men plus gear, rifles sticking out of windows, boots muddying the seats where passengers had sat only hours earlier. Drivers followed military officers instead of street maps, headlights dimmed, engines rattling along country roads normally used by farmers. Some taxis even kept their meters running out of habit, and the government later reimbursed the fares as if it had been an ordinary ride across town.

In purely military terms, the taxis didn't move enough troops to decide the battle by themselves. But psychologically, the image mattered enormously. Civilians and soldiers alike saw an entire city mobilizing, with everyday workers and their cars becoming part of the war effort overnight. Newspapers celebrated the "Taxis of the Marne" as a symbol of national unity, proof that even shopkeepers and cab drivers were now fighting the war.

165. Buried Alive in the Trenches

For many soldiers, the most frightening danger in the trenches didn't come from bullets or shrapnel at all, but from the earth itself. Dugouts, the small underground shelters carved into trench walls, were meant to be safe havens where men slept, wrote letters, or hid during bombardments. Some were shallow holes roofed with timber and sandbags. Others were dug 10–30 feet (3–9 meters) deep with wooden stairs, bunks, and candle shelves, looking almost like cramped underground bedrooms. But all of them depended on mud walls and rough beams for support, and under heavy shellfire, that wasn't enough.

When artillery struck nearby, the ground shook like an earthquake. Walls cracked. Dust rained from the ceiling. Then, without warning, entire sections collapsed. Tons of wet clay, timber, and sandbags poured down the stairwell, sealing exits in seconds. Men inside were often trapped before they even understood what had happened. Rescue was slow and desperate. Comrades clawed at the mud with shovels, helmets, or bare hands, racing against time while more shells continued to fall. Sometimes they reached their friends quickly. Often they didn't.

Many of the dead showed no wounds at all. Instead, they had simply suffocated. Air pockets vanished, candles went out, and the weight of soil crushed the space smaller and smaller until breathing became impossible. Survivors described hearing faint tapping or muffled shouting from underground that gradually faded. In some sectors, entire dugouts disappeared, burying a dozen or more men at once. After major bombardments, burial parties sometimes found bodies days later, still seated on benches or lying on bunks as if asleep.

Ironically, the deeper the dugout, the safer it seemed from shells, but the more deadly it became if it collapsed. Soldiers learned to fear heavy bombardments not just for the explosions above, but for the thought of being entombed below. Many later said they preferred taking their chances in the open trench rather than sleeping too deep underground.

166. When the French Army Refused to Attack

By 1917, the French army had been fighting almost continuously for nearly three years, and the strain was showing in every muddy trench. Hundreds of thousands were already dead from Verdun and the Somme, entire villages back home had lost their young men, and yet generals still promised that the next big offensive would finally end the war. In the spring of 1917, General Robert Nivelle launched exactly such a promise: a massive assault that he claimed would break the German lines within forty-eight hours. Instead, it turned into a slaughter. Machine guns and artillery tore apart the attacking waves. In just a few weeks, France suffered roughly

100,000–120,000 casualties for almost no ground. Survivors returned to the trenches furious and exhausted. They felt tricked, sacrificed for nothing, and asked to die again for the same result.

Then something rare and terrifying happened: the army didn't run from the enemy, it simply refused to move. Entire units obeyed defensive orders but would not go "over the top." Some companies stayed in their trenches and stacked their rifles. Others marched away singing protest songs or boarded trains without permission. In some sectors, soldiers shouted, "We'll defend France, but we won't attack." It wasn't chaos or revolution. It was quiet defiance. Men were done with suicidal assaults. At its peak, the unrest affected parts of nearly half the French divisions on the Western Front, tens of thousands of soldiers in total. For a moment, the French high command feared its own army might collapse completely.

The government kept the crisis secret, terrified the Germans might discover how fragile the line really was. Instead of mass executions, the new commander, Philippe Pétain, chose a different approach. He improved rations, increased leave, rotated exhausted units more often, and promised no more pointless attacks. Discipline still returned, but not without punishment: around 3,000 court-martials were held, hundreds sentenced to death, and roughly fifty actually executed as examples. The message was clear, mercy mixed with firmness. The mutinies faded, but the damage lingered. For nearly a year afterward, France avoided large offensives and mostly fought defensively, waiting for American troops to arrive. For the first time in the war, it had become obvious that the greatest threat wasn't always the enemy's guns, it was an army simply too exhausted to keep fighting.

167. When Armies Began to Break from Within

France wasn't the only country whose soldiers reached their limit. By 1917–1918, the strain of industrial warfare was cracking armies across Europe and beyond, sometimes more dangerously than enemy fire ever could. In Russia, the situation spiraled fastest. Years of defeat, hunger, and poor leadership shattered discipline entirely. Soldiers stopped saluting officers, formed their own "soldiers' committees," voted on whether to obey orders, and sometimes simply walked away from the front. Desertions reached into the hundreds of thousands. Some units even turned on their own commanders. Rifles meant for the Germans were pointed inward instead. The army didn't just mutiny, it dissolved, helping trigger the Russian Revolution and forcing Russia out of the war altogether.

Italy nearly followed. After the catastrophic defeat at Caporetto in 1917, entire formations collapsed in panic. Retreating soldiers threw away rifles, clogged roads, and fled for miles. Tens of thousands were captured, and others simply disappeared into the countryside. Officers responded brutally, with harsh discipline and executions meant to restore order. The line eventually stabilized, but trust between soldiers and commanders never fully recovered.

Britain avoided mass mutiny, but the strain still showed in quieter ways. There were strikes, refusals, and small protests over endless offensives and poor leave. Some exhausted units quietly resisted orders or delayed attacks. Colonial troops, especially from India, Africa, and the Caribbean, sometimes protested unequal treatment, lower pay, and racist discipline. A few refused labor assignments or demanded better conditions, reminding commanders that loyalty had limits. These were rarely called "mutinies" officially, but they revealed deep frustration beneath the surface.

Then came Germany's breaking point. By late 1918, food shortages were severe, cities were starving, and soldiers knew the war was lost. When German naval commanders ordered the fleet to sail for one last "glorious" suicide battle against Britain, the sailors refused outright. Ships stayed in harbor. Arrests triggered riots. The unrest spread from ports to factories to entire cities. Workers joined in. Flags changed. Within days, what began as a naval mutiny became a national revolution. The Kaiser abdicated, the government collapsed, and Germany asked for an armistice. The war ended not because its army was destroyed in battle, but because the country behind it simply stopped fighting. By the final year of the war, governments feared their own soldiers almost as much as the enemy.

THIRTEEN

Conclusion

World War I officially ended at the eleventh hour of the eleventh day of the eleventh month in 1918. The guns stopped. Soldiers climbed cautiously out of trenches. Church bells rang across Europe. Crowds flooded streets in Paris, London, and New York. After more than four years of industrial slaughter, the silence must have felt unreal. But the war did not truly end that morning. It simply changed form.

Empires that had ruled for centuries vanished almost overnight. The German, Austro-Hungarian, Ottoman, and Russian empires collapsed, redrawing the map of Europe and the Middle East in ways that would echo for generations. New nations appeared. Old borders disappeared. Political revolutions erupted. Entire economies staggered under debt and reconstruction. Millions of wounded men returned home to cities that no longer felt the same.

The human cost was almost beyond comprehension. Around 16–20 million people were dead. Tens of millions more were wounded. Some carried visible scars: missing limbs, damaged lungs, blinded eyes. Others carried invisible ones: nightmares, trembling hands, silence that never fully lifted. A whole generation had grown up in mud, noise, and loss. And yet, out of that destruction, the modern world took shape.

Air power, tanks, mass production, propaganda, daylight saving time, rationing systems, plastic surgery, blood banks, intelligence networks, global finance, women in heavy industry, psychological warfare; so many parts of the twentieth century were either born or transformed during those four years. Even everyday language changed. We still talk about "front lines," "campaigns," and "being in the trenches," often without realizing the phrases were forged in barbed wire and artillery smoke.

The war also shifted power across the globe. Europe emerged exhausted and indebted. The United States emerged richer and stronger. Colonial troops returned home with new expectations. Women who had run factories demanded a larger role in society. The seeds of future conflicts were planted in peace treaties that satisfied almost no one.

Perhaps the most haunting part is this: in 1914, millions believed the war would be short, glorious, and decisive. By 1918, the illusion of quick, clean war had shattered forever. World War I taught humanity that industrial conflict could consume entire nations, not just armies. It blurred the line between soldier and civilian. It proved that factories, farms, banks, and even clocks could become weapons.

World War I was once called "the war to end all wars." History proved otherwise. Yet understanding it remains essential. Not just for trivia nights or surprising facts, but because so much of our modern world, politically, economically, socially, and even linguistically, was shaped in those trenches.

Every statistic in this book hides a human story. Every innovation was born from urgency. Every strange detail, from trench slang to war bonds to blackout curtains, was part of a much larger transformation.

The war may have ended in 1918, but its shadow stretches across the century that followed.

And now, more than a hundred years later, we are still living in the world it created.

Bonus!

Thanks for supporting me and purchasing this book! I'd like to send you some freebies. They include:

- The digital version of *500 World War I & II Facts*

- The digital version of *101 Idioms and Phrases*

- The audiobook for my best seller *1144 Random Facts*

Scan the QR code below, enter your email and I'll send you all the files. Happy reading!